WISCONSIN STATE PARKS

BUCKET LIST

ISBN: 9798758862704
Copyright © 2022

Thank you for buying our book!
We hope you like it.

Your feedback is important to us, and we
would greatly appreciate it if you could take
a moment to share your thoughts by leaving
an online review.

Your review will not only help us improve as
an author but also assist other potential
readers in making informed decisions.

Once again, thank you for your support and
for considering leaving a review.

ABOUT WISCONSIN

Wisconsin became an American territory after the American Revolution and soon thereafter began attracting settlers seeking work in its mining, timber, and dairy industries. It was admitted to the union as the 30th state in 1848. In the years leading up to the Civil War, Wisconsin was an important stop on the Underground Railroad, with many slaves passing through the state on their way to freedom in Canada.

Today, Wisconsin is a leader in dairy production and is known for its high-quality cheddar cheese - residents sometimes refer to themselves as "cheeseheads." Famous Wisconsin residents include architect Frank Lloyd Wright, magician Harry Houdini, and U.S. Army General Douglas MacArthur.

More than 12,000 years ago, the area of present-day Wisconsin was covered by huge glaciers. During Wisconsin's glacial stage, when the ice sheet began to melt, it left behind scenic physical features, including sand plains, terminal and basin moraines, drumlins, oases, and low-lying areas that became lakes. In October 1871, the most destructive forest fire in American history broke out in Wisconsin: 1,200 people died and 2 billion trees burned in the fire known as the Great Peshtigo Fire. Wisconsin's climate is characterized by long, cold winters and warm, relatively short summers. Forests once covered more than four-fifths of the state, with the remainder being prairies and wetlands. Most of the forests have been cleared for timber and agricultural crops, but as a result of natural regrowth and reforestation, about two-fifths of Wisconsin is reforested.

About nine-tenths of Wisconsin's population comes from northern Europe. Those of German descent are the most numerous, followed by those of Irish, Polish, Scandinavian (mainly Norwegian), and British descent. African-Americans are the largest minority group in Wisconsin, making up about 6% of the population. Native Americans make up less than 1 percent of the population. There are towns with fewer than 1,000 residents throughout the state, but about two-thirds of Wisconsinites live in urban areas. Most people live in the Southeast, where eastern migrants first arrived and settled.

The three major economic enterprises of the state of Wisconsin are manufacturing, agriculture and tourism. Agriculture in Wisconsin is primarily based on intensive dairy production. Manufacturing is mainly engaged in the processing of agricultural products, as well as the production of metal products and forest products. Milwaukee and the surrounding area is one of the major manufacturing centers in the state, which in addition to brewing specializes in the production of electrical machinery and equipment. Tourism emerged as a major industry in the 1950s.

Wisconsin is a place where you can explore pristine lakes, miles of scenic hiking trails, and stunning natural wonders. About 120,000 acres (50,000 hectares) of state parks and millions of acres of national, state, and county forests are available for recreational use in the state of Wisconsin. Most of the public forests are in the north, although there is a park within an hour's drive of almost every place in the state. The sparsely populated, heavily forested northern Glacier region is the epitome of the Northwoods, with clear streams and hundreds of lakes for fishing and water sports. Whether you enjoy outdoor activities like hiking, biking, fishing, canoeing, or indoor activities like shopping, museums, and art galleries, you won't be disappointed.

Among the more interesting vacation areas is the Door Peninsula, between Lake Michigan and Green Bay, with miles of rocky coastline and sandy beaches and five state parks. It is largely forested, with summer cottages, small seaside villages, craft stores, and summer theater. One of the least known areas of the state, but deserving of more attention, is the scenic mountainous and valley country of the Western Highlands, with steep wooded slopes, bare rock cliffs and towers, tree-lined side roads winding through quiet pastoral scenes that include many Amish farms and the preserved homes of Cornish lead miners at Mineral Point and at Merrimac, the only surviving car ferry across the Wisconsin River.

A vacation in Wisconsin can put you close to the Kettle Moraine State Forest, which has excellent biking trails. Or choose Wisconsin's Apostle Islands - kayakers will love exploring Lake Superior's many caves and shipwrecks.

Food lovers will love to try as many Wisconsin artisan cheeses as possible. You can drive from cheesemaker to cheesemaker or choose to vacation in Wisconsin in a city with a good farmers market - then the cheesemakers will bring their wares to you. And what pairs better with craft cheeses than craft beer? In Milwaukee, take a tour and tasting at Lakefront and Sprecher breweries.

Wisconsin Dells is a classic family vacation destination. Wisconsin Dells vacations will put you close to all the action - you'll have to pry the kids away from the amusement parks, wave pools, and water parks in Wisconsin Dells!

Lake Geneva boasts clean beaches, golf, and a small-town atmosphere that is sure to appeal to city dwellers - it's a popular destination for Chicago residents.

INVENTORY

- ☐ BEAR SPRAY
- ☐ BINOCULARS
- ☐ CAMERA + ACCESSORIES
- ☐ CELL PHONE + CHARGER
- ☐ FIRST AID KIT
- ☐ FLASHLIGHT/ HEADLAMP
- ☐ FLEECE/ WATERPROOF JACKET
- ☐ GUIDE BOOK
- ☐ HAND LOTION
- ☐ HAND SANITIZER
- ☐ HIKING SHOES
- ☐ INSECT REPELLENT
- ☐ LIP BALM
- ☐ MEDICATIONS AND PAINKILLERS
- ☐ SUNGLASSES
- ☐ SNACKS
- ☐ SPARE SOCKS
- ☐ SUN HAT
- ☐ SUNSCREEN
- ☐ TOILET PAPER
- ☐ TRASH BAGS
- ☐ WALKING STICK
- ☐ WATER
- ☐ WATER SHOES/ SANDALS

PARK NAME	COUNTY	EST.	VISITED
Amnicon Falls State Park	Douglas	1961	
Aztalan State Park	Jefferson	1947	
Belmont Mound State Park	Lafayette	1961	
Big Bay State Park	Ashland	1963	
Big Foot Beach State Park	Walworth	1949	
Black River State Forest	Jackson	1957	
Blue Mound State Park	Dane	1959	
Brule River State Forest	Douglas	1907	
Brunet Island State Park	Chippewa	1936	
Buckhorn State Park	Juneau	1971	
Cadiz Springs State Recreation Area	Green	1970	
Capital Springs State Recreation Area	Dane	2000	
Chippewa Flowage	Sawyer	1923	
Chippewa Moraine State Recreation Area	Chippewa	1971	
Copper Culture State Park	Oconto	1959	
Copper Falls State Park	Ashland	1929	
Coulee Experimental State Forest	La Crosse	1960	
Council Grounds State Park	Lincoln	1938	
Cross Plains State Park	Dane	1971	
Devil's Lake State Park	Sauk	1911	
Fischer Creek State Recreation Area	Manitowoc	1991	
Flambeau River State Forest	Sawyer, Price	1930	
Governor Dodge State Park	Iowa	1948	
Governor Earl Peshtigo River State Forest	Marinette	2001	
Governor Knowles State Forest	Burnett, Polk	1970	
Governor Nelson State Park	Dane	1975	
Governor Thompson State Park	Marinette	2000	
Harrington Beach State Park	Ozaukee	1966	

PARK NAME	COUNTY	EST.	VISITED
Hartman Creek State Park	Waupaca	1962	
Havenwoods State Forest	Milwaukee	1979	
Heritage Hill State Park	Brown	1973	
High Cliff State Park	Calumet	1954	
Hoffman Hills State Recreation Area	Dunn	1980	
Interstate State Park	Polk	1900	
Kettle Moraine State Forest	Washington	1937	
Kinnickinnic State Park	Pierce	1972	
Kohler-Andrae State Park	Sheboygan	1928	
Lake Kegonsa State Park	Dane	1962	
Lake Wissota State Park	Chippewa	1962	
Lakeshore State Park	Milwaukee	1998	
Lost Dauphin State Park	Brown	1947	
Lower Wisconsin State Riverway	Grant, Boundary, Dane	1989	
MacKenzie Center	Columbia	1930	
Menominee River State Recreation Area	Marinette	2010	
Merrick State Park	Buffalo	1932	
Mill Bluff State Park	Monroe, Juneau	1936	
Mirror Lake State Park	Sauk	1962	
Natural Bridge State Park	Sauk	1972	
Nelson Dewey State Park	Grant	1935	
New Glarus Woods State Park	Green	1934	
Newport State Park	Door	1964	
Northern Highland American Legion State Forest	Vilas, Oneida, Iron	1925	
Pattison State Park	Douglas	1920	
Peninsula State Park	Door	1909	
Perrot State Park	Trempealeau	1918	
Point Beach State Forest	Manitowoc	1938	

PARK NAME	COUNTY	EST.	VISITED
Potawatomi State Park	Door	1928	
Rib Mountain State Park	Marathon	1927	
Richard Bong State Recreation Area	Kenosha	1963	
Roche-a-Cri State Park	Adams	1948	
Rock Island State Park	Door	1965	
Rocky Arbor State Park	Juneau	1932	
Sauk Prairie State Recreation Area	Sauk	2004	
Straight Lake State Park	Polk	2002	
Tower Hill State Park	Iowa	1922	
Turtle-Flambeau Scenic Waters Area	Iron	1926	
Whitefish Dunes State Park	Door	1967	
Wildcat Mountain State Park	Vernon	1948	
Willow River State Park	St. Croix	1967	
Wyalusing State Park	Grant	1917	
Yellowstone Lake State Park	Lafayette	1970	

COUNTY	PARK NAME	EST.	VISITED
Adams	Roche-a-Cri State Park	1948	
Ashland	Big Bay State Park	1963	
Ashland	Copper Falls State Park	1929	
Brown	Heritage Hill State Park	1973	
Brown	Lost Dauphin State Park	1947	
Buffalo	Merrick State Park	1932	
Burnett, Polk	Governor Knowles State Forest	1970	
Calumet	High Cliff State Park	1954	
Chippewa	Brunet Island State Park	1936	
Chippewa	Chippewa Moraine State Recreation Area	1971	
Chippewa	Lake Wissota State Park	1962	
Columbia	MacKenzie Center	1930	
Dane	Blue Mound State Park	1959	
Dane	Capital Springs State Recreation Area	2000	
Dane	Cross Plains State Park	1971	
Dane	Governor Nelson State Park	1975	
Dane	Lake Kegonsa State Park	1962	
Door	Newport State Park	1964	
Door	Peninsula State Park	1909	
Door	Potawatomi State Park	1928	
Door	Rock Island State Park	1965	
Door	Whitefish Dunes State Park	1967	
Douglas	Amnicon Falls State Park	1961	
Douglas	Brule River State Forest	1907	
Douglas	Pattison State Park	1920	
Dunn	Hoffman Hills State Recreation Area	1980	
Grant	Nelson Dewey State Park	1935	
Grant	Wyalusing State Park	1917	

COUNTY	PARK NAME	EST.	VISITED
Grant, Boundary, Dane	Lower Wisconsin State Riverway	1989	
Green	Cadiz Springs State Recreation Area	1970	
Green	New Glarus Woods State Park	1934	
Iowa	Governor Dodge State Park	1948	
Iowa	Tower Hill State Park	1922	
Iron	Turtle-Flambeau Scenic Waters Area	1926	
Jackson	Black River State Forest	1957	
Jefferson	Aztalan State Park	1947	
Juneau	Buckhorn State Park	1971	
Juneau	Rocky Arbor State Park	1932	
Kenosha	Richard Bong State Recreation Area	1963	
La Crosse	Coulee Experimental State Forest	1960	
Lafayette	Belmont Mound State Park	1961	
Lafayette	Yellowstone Lake State Park	1970	
Lincoln	Council Grounds State Park	1938	
Maintowoc	Point Beach State Forest	1938	
Manitowoc	Fischer Creek State Recreation Area	1991	
Marathon	Rib Mountain State Park	1927	
Marinette	Governor Thompson State Park	2000	
Marinette	Menominee River State Recreation Area	2010	
Marinette	Governor Earl Peshtigo River State Forest	2001	
Milwaukee	Havenwoods State Forest	1979	
Milwaukee	Lakeshore State Park	1998	
Monroe, Juneau	Mill Bluff State Park	1936	
Oconto	Copper Culture State Park	1959	
Ozaukee	Harrington Beach State Park	1966	
Pierce	Kinnickinnic State Park	1972	
Polk	Interstate State Park	1900	

COUNTY	PARK NAME	EST.	VISITED
Polk	Straight Lake State Park	2002	
Sauk	Devil's Lake State Park	1911	
Sauk	Mirror Lake State Park	1962	
Sauk	Natural Bridge State Park	1972	
Sauk	Sauk Prairie State Recreation Area	2004	
Sawyer	Chippewa Flowage	1923	
Sawyer, Price	Flambeau River State Forest	1930	
Sheboygan	Kohler-Andrae State Park	1928	
St. Croix	Willow River State Park	1967	
Trempealeau	Perrot State Park	1918	
Vernon	Wildcat Mountain State Park	1948	
Vilas, Oneida, Iron	Northern Highland American Legion State Forest	1925	
Walworth	Big Foot Beach State Park	1949	
Washington	Kettle Moraine State Forest	1937	
Waupaca	Hartman Creek State Park	1962	

1. Amnicon Falls State Park
2. Aztalan State Park
3. Belmont Mound State Park
4. Big Bay State Park
5. Big Foot Beach State Park
6. Black River State Forest
7. Blue Mound State Park
8. Brule River State Forest
9. Brunet Island State Park
10. Buckhorn State Park
11. Cadiz Springs State Recreation Area
12. Capital Springs State Recreation Area
13. Chippewa Flowage
14. Chippewa Moraine State Recreation Area
15. Copper Culture State Park
16. Copper Falls State Park
17. Coulee Experimental State Forest
18. Council Grounds State Park
19. Cross Plains State Park
20. Devil's Lake State Park
21. Fischer Creek State Recreation Area
22. Flambeau River State Forest
23. Governor Dodge State Park
24. Governor Earl Peshtigo River State Forest
25. Governor Knowles State Forest
26. Governor Nelson State Park
27. Governor Thompson State Park
28. Harrington Beach State Park
29. Hartman Creek State Park
30. Havenwoods State Forest
31. Heritage Hill State Park
32. High Cliff State Park
33. Hoffman Hills State Recreation Area
34. Interstate State Park
35. Kettle Moraine State Forest
36. Kinnickinnic State Park
37. Kohler-Andrae State Park
38. Lake Kegonsa State Park
39. Lake Wissota State Park
40. Lakeshore State Park
41. Lost Dauphin State Park
42. Lower Wisconsin State Riverway
43. MacKenzie Center
44. Menominee River State Recreation Area
45. Merrick State Park
46. Mill Bluff State Park
47. Mirror Lake State Park
48. Natural Bridge State Park
49. Nelson Dewey State Park
50. New Glarus Woods State Park
51. Newport State Park
52. Northern Highland American Legion State Forest
53. Pattison State Park
54. Peninsula State Park
55. Perrot State Park
56. Point Beach State Forest
57. Potawatomi State Park
58. Rib Mountain State Park
59. Richard Bong State Recreation Area
60. Roche-a-Cri State Park
61. Rock Island State Park
62. Rocky Arbor State Park
63. Sauk Prairie State Recreation Area
64. Straight Lake State Park
65. Tower Hill State Park
66. Turtle-Flambeau Scenic Waters Area
67. Whitefish Dunes State Park
68. Wildcat Mountain State Park
69. Willow River State Park
70. Wyalusing State Park
71. Yellowstone Lake State Park

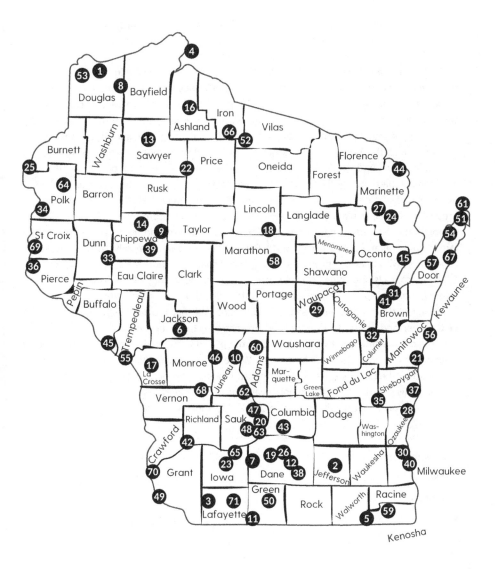

AMNICON FALLS STATE PARK

COUNTY	ESTABLISHED	AREA (AC/HA)
DOUGLAS	1961	825 / 334

The park is situated in the southern part of Wisconsin, to the southeast of the town of Superior. It's home to a sequence of waterfalls on the Amnicon River, which meanders around a small island and passes beneath a historic covered bridge. These waterfalls are split into upper and lower sections, and visitors are welcome to swim in both areas. The park offers 2.9 miles of trails that run alongside both sides of the river, and there's even a snowshoe trail that leads to more remote parts of the park, where you can enjoy snowshoeing and winter hiking. During winter, there's a designated 1.5-mile snowshoe trail. The park provides a great setting for picnicking, camping, hiking in the woods, and learning about the Douglas Fault, a geological formation responsible for creating the waterfalls. You'll find three picnic areas along the river near the park office, and there are picnic tables and grills available in the parking area near the covered bridge. Amnicon Falls State Park has 36 camping sites, including one that's handicapped accessible, as well as two hiking sites located 100 and 150 feet from the parking lot. The campground features swings, a sandbox, and a large playground, making it perfect for family enjoyment. Amnicon Falls State Park offers a tranquil, mostly rustic camping experience, with tall trees providing partial or full shade to all the sites. The park boasts 1.8 miles of trails, including several short ones along both sides of the Amnicon River, offering various perspectives of the waterfalls and the surrounding landscape. Additionally, there's a 0.8-mile self-guided nature trail that provides picturesque views of the river and access to the riverbed downstream from the falls area. Hunting and trapping are permitted in the open areas of the park during the designated hunting and trapping season in Wisconsin state parks. While the Amnicon River is more renowned for its scenic beauty than its angling opportunities, it can occasionally yield excellent catches. This warm stream flows northward into Lake Superior, and below the park, it transitions from a fast-flowing river to a slow, wide, meandering one.

DATE(S) VISITED .... □ SPRING □ SUMMER □ FALL □ WINTER

LODGING .... □ ☼ □ ☁ □ ☁ □ ☁ □ ☁

WHO I WENT WITH .... FEE(S) .... PARK HOURS .... TEMP:.........

WILL I RETURN? YES / NO   RATING ☆ ☆ ☆ ☆ ☆

NOTES

AZTALAN STATE PARK

COUNTY	ESTABLISHED	AREA (AC/HA)
JEFFERSON	1947	172 / 70

This park holds the prestigious title of being a National Historic Landmark and is home to one of the most significant archaeological sites in Wisconsin. Aztalan is the location of an ancient settlement that was part of the Mississippian culture, thriving between the 10th and 13th centuries. The indigenous inhabitants constructed massive earthen mounds for both religious and political purposes. They were part of a widespread culture with significant settlements scattered across the Mississippi Valley and its various tributaries. Their extensive trade network stretched from the Great Lakes to the Gulf Coast and throughout the southeastern region of what is now the United States. Within the park, you can find reconstructions of fragments of a palisade and two mounds. The park offers two miles of trails that wind through open prairies and alongside the Crawfish River. The park is predominantly an open prairie, with 38 out of its 172 acres covered by oak woodlands. Visitors have the opportunity to kayak, boat, and fish for northern pike, catfish, and zander in the Crawfish River. Picnicking is also allowed in the park, and there's an open shelter that can be reserved for your convenience. During the winter, cross-country skiing and snowshoeing are permitted, although the trails are not regularly maintained. Please note that sledding is not allowed in the park, and it's illegal to sled on the mounds.

DATE(S) VISITED .... ☐ SPRING ☐ SUMMER ☐ FALL ☐ WINTER

LODGING .... ☐ ☀ ☐ ☁ ☐ 🌧 ☐ 🌬 ☐ ❄

WHO I WENT WITH .... FEE(S) .... PARK HOURS .... TEMP:.........

WILL I RETURN? YES / NO   RATING ☆ ☆ ☆ ☆ ☆

NOTES

PASSPORT STAMPS

BELMONT MOUND STATE PARK

COUNTY	ESTABLISHED	AREA (AC/HA)
LAFAYETTE	1961	274 / 111

The park encompasses Belmont Mound, a 1,400-foot hill crowned with a 64-foot high observation tower. This wooded mound is teeming with berries and wildlife. The name "Belmont" has French origins, meaning "beautiful mountain." An additional eighty acres located in the northwest corner of the park have been designated as the Belmont Mound Woods State Natural Area. Within the park, there are 2.5 miles of hiking trails that wind around the base of the mound, cut through the center of the park, and form a loop in the northeast corner. While primarily intended for hiking, off-road bikes are also permitted to use these trails. Belmont Mound State Park offers year-round outdoor recreational opportunities for its visitors. Notably, the historic site of Wisconsin's First Capitol is situated just half a mile to the west of the park, and it's managed by the Belmont Lions Club. Hunting and trapping are allowed in the park's open areas during the designated hunting and trapping season for Wisconsin state parks. However, trapping is prohibited in closed areas, as indicated on the park's hunting map, and within a 100-yard radius of any designated use area, including trails. There's also a picnic area near the park's entrance, complete with some playground equipment. The park remains open throughout the year for snowshoeing and winter hiking, although the trails are not groomed for skiing.

DATE(S) VISITED .... ☐ SPRING ☐ SUMMER ☐ FALL ☐ WINTER

LODGING .... ☐ ☀ ☐ ☁ ☐ 🌧 ☐ 🌦 ☐ ❄

WHO I WENT WITH .... FEE(S) .... PARK HOURS .... TEMP:.........

WILL I RETURN? YES / NO   RATING ☆ ☆ ☆ ☆ ☆

NOTES

PASSPORT STAMPS

BIG BAY STATE PARK

COUNTY	ESTABLISHED	AREA (AC/HA)
ASHLAND	1963	2,350 / 951

Situated on Madeline Island, the largest among the 22 Apostle Islands in Lake Superior, this park showcases picturesque bluffs, sandstone caves, and a splendid 1.5-mile long sandy beach perfect for sunbathing. It's important to note that pets and fires are not allowed on the Big Bay State Park beach. The park lacks a boat launch, so many visitors opt to bring their canoes and kayaks, carrying them to the beach for launching. From the beach, you can paddle around the bay and the lagoon or explore the sea caves along the point. Anglers can try their luck catching northern pike in the park's lagoon and various species of trout in Lake Superior. The park is enveloped by unique habitat types, including Lakeside dunes, peat bogs, and old-growth forest. Bald eagles are a recurring sight in the park, returning annually to nest and rear their young. Additionally, Big Bay State Park boasts a 1-mile boardwalk, hiking trails, a spacious family campground, and two group camps, offering a total of 60 campsites. The day-use area provides picnic tables, grills, drinking water, and restrooms. To reach the park, you'll need to take a ferry from Bayfield to Madeline Island. The park boasts over 9 miles of trails, including nature trails, although bicycles are not permitted on any of the trails or boardwalks. Big Bay State Park remains open year-round, primarily attracting hunters, snow hikers, and cross-country skiers during the winter months. Nearby Bayfield and Madeline Island offer additional activities such as bus tours, golfing, art galleries, marinas, and the historic La Pointe Indian Burial Grounds, a site originally inhabited by the Ojibway (Chippewa) Indians. Bird enthusiasts will find the island park particularly captivating, with an extensive list of 240 bird species observed in the park, available at the park office. Moreover, there's a wildlife observation deck located along the east shore of the lagoon. As for hunting and trapping, they are permitted in the open areas of the park during the designated Wisconsin state parks hunting and trapping season. However, trapping is restricted in closed areas, as indicated on the park's hunting map, and within a 100-yard radius of any designated use area, including trails.

DATE(S) VISITED .... ☐ SPRING ☐ SUMMER ☐ FALL ☐ WINTER

LODGING .... ☐ ☀ ☐ ☁ ☐ 🌧 ☐ ⛅ ☐ ❄

WHO I WENT WITH .... FEE(S) .... PARK HOURS .... TEMP:.........

WILL I RETURN? YES / NO   RATING ☆ ☆ ☆ ☆ ☆

NOTES

BIG FOOT BEACH STATE PARK

COUNTY	ESTABLISHED	AREA (AC/HA)
WALWORTH	1949	271 / 110

This park is situated along the shores of Lake Geneva and takes its name from Chief Big Foot of the Potawatomi tribe. It's a destination known for a variety of popular attractions, including hiking, swimming, boating, camping, and fishing. The park offers a range of hiking trails, which are generally short and vary in difficulty, from easy to moderate. Lake Geneva is celebrated for its pristine, crystal-clear waters, and at Big Foot Beach, there's a designated 100-foot swimming area. Visitors can also explore the waters via kayaks and canoes available in Ceylon Lagoon and Lake Geneva. While the park doesn't have rental shops on-site, you can rent equipment from a local vendor located south of the park entrance. For those with boats, it's important to note that there's no boat launch within the park, but two public launches can be found to the south, one in downtown Lake Geneva and another in Linn Township. The north shoreline of the park is a popular spot for anchoring and enjoying a relaxing day by the water. Keep in mind that there are no lifeguards on duty. In addition to these water-based activities, the park boasts 5 miles of hiking trails, a family campground, a swimming beach, and picnic and playground areas. During the winter, snowshoeing and cross-country skiing are popular recreational options. Big Foot Beach State Park provides a total of 100 campsites. The upper loop campsites come equipped with gravel pads, fire rings, and picnic tables. Among them, 34 sites have electric pedestals for added convenience. The campground also features amenities such as a dump station, vault toilets, and a shower building. For campers' convenience, firewood, ice, and fire starters can be purchased at the camp host site located near the campground entrance.

DATE(S) VISITED .... □ SPRING □ SUMMER □ FALL □ WINTER

LODGING .... □☼ □☁ □☔ □☁ □❄

WHO I WENT WITH .... FEE(S) .... PARK HOURS .... TEMP:.........

WILL I RETURN? YES / NO   RATING ☆ ☆ ☆ ☆ ☆

NOTES

PASSPORT STAMPS

BLACK RIVER STATE FOREST

COUNTY	ESTABLISHED	AREA (AC/HA)
JACKSON	1957	68,000 / 27,842

This forest encompasses a landscape where two branches of the Black River wind their way through, surrounded by a mix of pine and oak trees, and framed by towering sandstone pillars. Positioned at the geographical heart of Wisconsin, this property presents a wealth of recreational possibilities, including camping, kayaking, hunting, hiking, skiing, and ATV riding. The Black River State Forest boasts an extensive network of 24 miles of trails that wind through a visually captivating range of hills, cliffs, and bluffs, all set within a mature pine forest. The Nordic trail system, renowned for its quality, is often considered one of Wisconsin's finest. Additionally, there are 29 miles of biking trails, with five of them situated at the Pigeon Creek campground. For camping enthusiasts, the forest offers a variety of camping options, including family campgrounds at Castle Mound, East Fork, and Pigeon Creek, along with group camping within the forest and primitive camping opportunities. All three campgrounds (Castle Mound, East Fork, and Pigeon Creek) come equipped with picnic facilities, including hand pumps for water, picnic tables, grills, and restrooms. Castle Mound and Pigeon Creek campgrounds also feature playgrounds and are handicapped accessible, while Perry Creek and Oxbow Pond have more limited picnic amenities, such as picnic tables and grills. The Black River and the East Fork of the Black River provide fantastic opportunities for kayaking. The East Fork, in particular, offers a scenic river experience with a gentle current and moderately rocky terrain. It's important to note that paddling on the East Fork is not recommended when water levels are low. Visitors to the forest might even encounter elk roaming the area. Elk were reintroduced to the region in 2015 and 2016 after being absent for over 125 years. For those interested in fishing, access to the forest's lakes, waterways, and the Black River can be found at numerous locations, mainly through boat launches and fishing piers. Lastly, the Black River State Forest is an excellent destination for hunting, being open to public hunting during designated seasons with the appropriate license.

DATE(S) VISITED ....

LODGING ....

WHO I WENT WITH ....

WILL I RETURN? YES / NO

☐ SPRING ☐ SUMMER ☐ FALL ☐ WINTER

☐ ☀ ☐ ☁ ☐ 🌧 ☐ ⛈ ☐ ❄

FEE(S) .... PARK HOURS .... TEMP:........

RATING ☆ ☆ ☆ ☆ ☆

NOTES

BLUE MOUND STATE PARK

COUNTY	ESTABLISHED	AREA (AC/HA)
DANE	1959	1,153 / 467

Perched atop the highest point in the southern region of Wisconsin, Blue Mound State Park boasts breathtaking vistas and distinctive geological formations. The park is home to a pair of observation towers that provide stunning views in various directions. To the north, you can observe the Wisconsin River valley and the Baraboo Range. To the south and west, the landscape unfolds to reveal mounds, buttes, and rolling forests characteristic of the Driftless Area. To the east, you'll take in the young glacial plains and the city of Madison. Blue Mound State Park offers more than 20 miles of picturesque trails that cater to hiking, off-road biking, and cross-country skiing. The park also features a family campground and grants access to the Military Ridge State Trail, which includes designated bicycle campsites. As a result, Blue Mound attracts visitors year-round. While all the park's trails are open to hiking, there are three specific trails exclusively designated for hiking in the spring, summer, and fall: the Indian Marker Tree Trail, the self-guided Flintrock Nature Trail, and the Pleasure Valley Hiking Trail. Additionally, there are 15.5 miles of challenging, off-road singletrack bike trails within the park. Bicyclists aged 16 and older must possess a state bicycle card in addition to a vehicle admission sticker. These trails are open during the spring, summer, and fall, except in wet conditions when they are closed for use. During winter, the trails are closed. Blue Mound State Park's campground is open throughout the year, providing 77 wooded campsites, 12 bike/hike-in sites, and a rustic cabin that is accessible to people with disabilities. The park's picnic area is another inviting space, offering opportunities for relaxation and recreation. Play equipment and sandboxes are available in the picnic area near the shelters and in the campground. Adjacent to the picnic area, you'll find a nature center with wildlife exhibits. Naturalists also conduct summer programs for visitors to enjoy. During the summer season, one of the park's most popular attractions is the 1,950-square foot swimming pool and the outdoor-themed splash pad, operating from Memorial Day to Labor Day. For outdoor enthusiasts, hunting and trapping are permitted in the open areas of the park during the designated Wisconsin state parks hunting and trapping season. However, trapping is restricted in closed areas as indicated on the park's hunting map and within a 100-yard radius of any designated use area, including trails. Snowshoeing is permitted throughout the park, with the exception of the cross-country ski trails.

DATE(S) VISITED .... ☐ SPRING ☐ SUMMER ☐ FALL ☐ WINTER

LODGING .... ☐ ☀ ☐ ☁ ☐ 🌧 ☐ 🌨 ☐ ❄

WHO I WENT WITH .... FEE(S) .... PARK HOURS .... TEMP:........

WILL I RETURN? YES / NO   RATING ☆ ☆ ☆ ☆ ☆

NOTES

PASSPORT STAMPS

BRULE RIVER STATE FOREST

COUNTY	ESTABLISHED	AREA (AC/HA)
DOUGLAS	1907	47,000 / 19,020

The Brule River State Forest offers a wide array of outstanding recreational opportunities, including activities like river paddling, trout fishing, wildlife observation, a 23-mile segment of the North Country National Scenic Trail, and access to 9 miles of Lake Superior shoreline. The entire 44-mile stretch of the Bois Brule River flows through the forest, enveloped by a natural woodland setting. For campers and nature enthusiasts, the forest provides two campgrounds that cater to family camping and offer convenient access to canoeing adventures on the Bois Brule River. This northern Wisconsin river is ideal for a leisurely float with the family, as well as an exhilarating ride through rapids. The upper river, particularly the stretch from Stones Bridge to Winneboujou, is perfect for a relaxed river trip that can be managed by nearly anyone. For those seeking a more thrilling experience, continuing on the river for an additional 45 minutes will bring you to the Little Joe Rapids, a modest class II rapids located just upstream of the Bois Brule canoe landing. If you don't have your own canoe or kayak, there's a canoe rental business in Brule that offers both equipment and guided trips, as well as pick-up and drop-off services. The Brule River is renowned as one of Wisconsin's most picturesque and famous trout streams. Thanks to its generous size, highly productive fishery, and consistent flow of cool spring water, the Brule River is recognized as one of the premier trout streams in the Lake States. Both the Bois Brule and Copper Range campgrounds offer reservable campsites for visitors. Within the forest, you can also find the Cedar Island Lodge, known as the "Summer White House," where numerous American presidents and generals have spent their vacations. The state forest attracts kayakers and cross-country skiers, offering a range of opportunities for outdoor recreation. The Stoney Hill nature trail, a 1.7-mile loop that commences at the Bois Brule Campground, provides a scenic hike. Along the trail, you'll find exhibits that shed light on the forest's natural and cultural history. While the trail has some steep sections, reaching the viewpoint at the top of Stony Hill offers a pleasant break and a breathtaking view of the Brule River Valley. Keep in mind that pets are not allowed on the nature trail. For horseback riders, there are multiple trails within the Brule River State Forest, including the Brule-St. Croix Snowmobile Trail, hiking trails suitable for hunters, and numerous forest roads. The North Country Trail, however, is exclusively for foot traffic, and horses are not permitted on it. Hunters will also find ample opportunities within the forest, which features over 40 miles of hunter walking trails that provide convenient access to prime habitat for a variety of game animals. Commonly hunted species include deer and grouse, but there are also hunting opportunities for woodcock, bear, and waterfowl.

BRUNET ISLAND STATE PARK

COUNTY	ESTABLISHED	AREA (AC/HA)
CHIPPEWA	1936	1,303 / 496

Tranquil lagoons and meandering channels offer ideal settings for canoeing and observing wildlife. The rolling terrain of Chippewa County is a result of the last ice age, shaping the landscape of the area. The park is connected to the Old Abe State Trail, which stretches from Cornell to Chippewa Falls. Facilities within the park include 69 campsites, a picnic area, access to electricity, shelters, restrooms, playgrounds, a sports field, a swimming beach, and a network of hiking trails. In the winter months, the park also provides cross-country ski trails for winter sports enthusiasts. Nearby vendors in Cornell offer groceries, propane, fuel, and other camping supplies, while laundromats are available on Bridge and Main streets. Visitors can rent canoes and kayaks from local vendors. Bicycles are permitted on park roads and trails, with the exception of the Jean Brunet Nature Trail. The park's main 2-mile road features a designated lane for both bicyclists and pedestrians. Anglers of all ages can borrow basic fishing equipment free of charge from the park office. The park offers a variety of fishing opportunities, allowing you to catch a wide range of fish, including northern pike, walleye, smallmouth bass, catfish, crappie, muskie, and yellow perch. There are accessible fishing piers located near both the north and south camp areas. It's important to note that a Wisconsin fishing license is required for fishing within the park. Brunet Island encompasses nearly 20 acres of picnic area, situated on the south and west sides of the island. This area offers picturesque views of the Chippewa River and the surrounding countryside. A playground and a ball diamond can be found at the southeast end of the picnic area. For hunting and trapping enthusiasts, the park permits these activities in the open areas of the park during the designated Wisconsin state parks hunting and trapping season. However, trapping is not allowed in closed areas, as indicated on the park's hunting map or within a 100-yard radius of any designated use area, including trails. The island is situated within a stretch of water extending approximately 3.5 to 4 miles from the Cornell dam to the Holcombe dam. This area offers excellent flat water paddling opportunities, with numerous channels winding through undeveloped islands in the northern section of the park.

DATE(S) VISITED ....

☐ SPRING   ☐ SUMMER   ☐ FALL   ☐ WINTER

LODGING ....

☐ ☀   ☐ ☁   ☐ 🌧   ☐ 🌊   ☐ ❄

WHO I WENT WITH ....

FEE(S) .... PARK HOURS .... TEMP:.........

WILL I RETURN? YES / NO

RATING ☆ ☆ ☆ ☆ ☆

NOTES

BUCKHORN STATE PARK

COUNTY	ESTABLISHED	AREA (AC/HA)
JUNEAU	1971	8,190 / 2,830

Buckhorn State Park is a haven for those who cherish water-based activities, hunting, hiking, camping, and the wonders of nature. The park provides family and group campsites, a canoe trail, and a fishing pier for visitors to enjoy. It's located on a peninsula within Castle Rock Lake, which is a reservoir formed at the confluence of the Wisconsin and Yellow rivers. The park's landscape is characterized by sandy soil left behind by receding glaciers. Explorers have the opportunity to traverse 7 miles of trails, each offering a unique experience. These trails include paths leading to a fish pond specifically designed for young anglers, a geocaching trail, and one featuring a 20-foot observation tower. During the winter, five miles of trails are groomed to accommodate cross-country skiing. Buckhorn State Park offers two picnic areas equipped with grills, tables, water pumps, picnic shelters, and playground equipment, all of which can be reserved for gatherings. Additionally, the park connects to the 1,600-acre Buckhorn Wildlife Area and the adjacent 2,200-acre Yellow River Wildlife Area. These areas provide additional opportunities for recreation, including various hunting seasons and access to the Castle Rock Flowage. The open waters of the Castle Rock Flowage are a playground for a wide range of watercraft. You'll see everything from bass boats, sailboats, and ski boats to pontoon boats, jet skis, and even houseboats. The park and wildlife area feature five boat ramps, and there's a canoe launch on the eastern side of the peninsula, leading to a peaceful slough that connects to the main part of the flowage. In-season, canoe and kayak rentals are available through the Friends of Buckhorn State Park, and there's a specially adapted kayak for individuals with disabilities. The Castle Rock Flowage is renowned for its excellent fishing opportunities, offering a diverse range of fish species that ensure year-round angling excitement at numerous spots. For bank fishing, some of the best locations include the 90-foot fishing pier at the north picnic area, the bank at the Buckhorn Bridge, and the shoreline at the kayak landing. Hunting and trapping are permitted in the open areas of the park during the designated Wisconsin state parks hunting and trapping season, with trapping being restricted in closed areas, as indicated on the park's hunting map, and within 100 yards of any designated use area, including trails. During the winter, many hikers enjoy exploring the trails on skis, and the relatively flat terrain makes the trails suitable for family outings. When there's enough snow, approximately 6.5 miles of trails are groomed for cross-country skiing.

DATE(S) VISITED .... ☐ SPRING ☐ SUMMER ☐ FALL ☐ WINTER

LODGING .... ☐ ☀ ☐ ☁ ☐ 🌧 ☐ 🌊 ☐ ❄

WHO I WENT WITH .... FEE(S) .... PARK HOURS .... TEMP:.........

WILL I RETURN? YES / NO   RATING ☆ ☆ ☆ ☆ ☆

PASSPORT STAMPS

CADIZ SPRINGS STATE RECREATION AREA

COUNTY	ESTABLISHED	AREA (AC/HA)
GREEN	1970	645 / 261

Cadiz Springs serves as a day-use area, welcoming visitors for picnicking, hiking, hunting, fishing, and wildlife observation. Situated in southwestern Wisconsin, this region boasts a landscape that distinguishes it from the rest of the state. The Cadiz Springs State Recreation Area provides a range of outdoor recreational opportunities for nature enthusiasts throughout the year. The park features an extensive network of hiking trails, totaling 8 miles, which offer some of the finest spots to observe a diverse array of wildlife in their natural habitats, including forests, meadows, and aquatic environments. In this area, the swamps, marshes, and numerous lakes that were once present have given way to rolling hills and valleys, enriched by spring-fed streams. It's important to note that camping is not permitted at Cadiz Springs. For day visitors, Cadiz Springs offers picnic areas equipped with various grills and picnic tables. Additionally, there are two spacious open shelters within the park, both of which are equipped with lighting and electricity. Swimming enthusiasts can make use of the 150-foot sand beach at Cadiz Springs. The park encompasses two lakes, Beckman Lake and Zander Lake, which together cover an area of 93 acres. Beckman Lake features a boat launch, while Zander Lake is accessible for canoes and kayaks. It's important to be aware that both lakes have restrictions allowing the use of electric motors only. Fishing is a highly popular activity in this area, with a variety of warm and cold-water fish species available. Both lakes are home to abundant populations of bass and panfish, providing an enjoyable challenge for anglers who frequent these recreational waters. The lakes are stocked with brown and rainbow trout, northern pike, catfish, and whitehead. During the winter season, Cadiz Springs State Recreation Area is open for cross-country skiing, although the trails are not groomed. Visitors can also engage in snowshoeing, winter hiking, sledding, and snowmobiling in designated areas of the park. For hunting and trapping enthusiasts, the property permits these activities during the legally designated hunting and trapping seasons.

DATE(S) VISITED ....

□ SPRING   □ SUMMER   □ FALL   □ WINTER

LODGING ....

□ ☀   □ ☁   □ 🌧   □ 🌨   □ ✲

WHO I WENT WITH ....

FEE(S) ....   PARK HOURS ....   TEMP:.........

WILL I RETURN? YES / NO

RATING ☆ ☆ ☆ ☆ ☆

NOTES

CAPITAL SPRINGS STATE RECREATION AREA

COUNTY	ESTABLISHED	AREA (AC/HA)
DANE	2000	3,000 / 1,200

Just a short drive from downtown Madison, the Capital Springs State Recreation Area and Lake Farm Park in Dane County offer a wide range of recreational opportunities, including camping, hiking and skiing trails, picnicking, fishing, and boat launching on Lake Waubesa. You'll find multiple spacious picnic areas and playgrounds near Lake Waubesa, and three shelters within the area can be reserved for gatherings. The options for outdoor activities extend to wildlife viewing, cross-country skiing, snowshoeing, canoeing, and hunting. In the winter, 6 miles of trails are meticulously groomed for cross-country skiing, providing a snowy playground for winter enthusiasts. The boat launch remains accessible year-round, although each vehicle parked in the boat launch area must possess a lake access permit. Fishing is another popular activity within Lake Waubesa, and fishing licenses are a requirement for anglers. Additionally, Dane County's Lake Farm Park, located adjacent to Capital Springs, provides camping facilities. Capital Springs boasts over 6 miles of hiking trails and walking paths. Some of these trails are enhanced with interpretive signs along the way, offering hikers a chance to learn more about the area's natural features. Thanks to its diverse range of natural habitats, the park is an excellent location for birdwatching year-round. The Capital Springs State Trail traverses through the Capital Springs State Recreation Area, with direct access available at the campground in Lake Farm County Park near the Lussier Family Heritage Center. This paved trail is particularly popular among cyclists and also links to several other Madison city and state trails. Along the border of the Capital Springs Recreation Area, you'll discover numerous parks, trails, and points of natural interest. For hunting and trapping enthusiasts, the park permits these activities in the open areas during the designated Wisconsin state parks hunting and trapping seasons.

DATE(S) VISITED ....

□ SPRING □ SUMMER □ FALL □ WINTER

LODGING ....

□ ☀ □ ☁ □ 🌧 □ ⛅ □ ❄

WHO I WENT WITH ....

FEE(S) .... PARK HOURS .... TEMP:.........

WILL I RETURN? YES / NO

RATING ☆ ☆ ☆ ☆ ☆

NOTES

CHIPPEWA FLOWAGE

COUNTY	ESTABLISHED	AREA (AC/HA)
SAWYER	1923	15,300 / 6,197

The damming of the Chippewa River resulted in the confluence of waters from 11 natural lakes, 9 rivers, and numerous streams. There are six public access points for boaters to reach the Chippewa Flowage: four are provided by the DNR, one by the Lac Courte Oreilles Tribe (LCO), and one by the Town of Hayward. Boaters should exercise caution due to changing canal conditions, especially fluctuating water levels. Along the water's edge, you can encounter a variety of wildlife, including deer, bears, herons, otters, eagles, beavers, and even elk. The Chippewa Flowage is renowned for its unique Northwoods fishery, housing a diverse array of species. Anglers can find walleye, northern pike, large and smallmouth bass, crappie, bluegill, and perch in abundance. This location is perfect for quiet recreational activities such as kayaking, canoeing, birdwatching, hiking, and cross-country skiing. The area also boasts around a dozen golf courses for enthusiasts of the sport. Visitors have access to 18 primitive camping sites on the island, which are available for public use. Some of these sites are allocated on a first-come, first-served basis, while others can be reserved in advance. Each public campground is clearly marked with a sign and provides essential amenities like a fire pit, picnic table, and outdoor latrine. Camping is restricted to designated campgrounds, and all campsites are accessible solely by water. Some campsites may be closed or relocated periodically to facilitate vegetation regrowth, protect endangered species, or preserve sensitive habitats. Private resorts in the area also offer campsite options. On DNR land on the north side of the flowage, there are 2 miles of hiking and skiing trails, which can be reached through a parking area adjacent to County Highway B, located between Moss Creek and Hay Creek.

DATE(S) VISITED ....

LODGING ....

WHO I WENT WITH ....

WILL I RETURN? YES / NO

☐ SPRING   ☐ SUMMER   ☐ FALL   ☐ WINTER

☐ ☀   ☐ ☁   ☐ ☔   ☐ ☁   ☐ ❄

FEE(S) .... PARK HOURS .... TEMP:.........

RATING ☆ ☆ ☆ ☆ ☆

NOTES

PASSPORT STAMPS

CHIPPEWA MORAINE STATE RECREATION AREA

COUNTY	ESTABLISHED	AREA (AC/HA)
CHIPPEWA	1971	3,568 / 1,324

The Chippewa Moraine State Recreation Area, situated along the Ice Age National Scenic Trail, presents unspoiled natural beauty featuring kettle lakes and a multitude of glacial features. The Ice Age National Scenic Trail courses through the Chippewa Moraine, connecting to the interpretive center, loop trails, and three primitive, outpost campsites. This extensive trail system stretches over 1,000 miles, tracing the boundary of Wisconsin's last continental glacier. The woods within the Chippewa Moraine are primarily composed of mature maple and pine trees. The Chippewa Moraine segment of the Ice Age National Scientific Reserve encompasses 23 miles of trails, exclusively designated for hikers. Motorized vehicles, horses, and mountain bikes are not permitted within the Chippewa Moraine. The trail network is well-maintained, offering various route options for visitors. Popular activities include hiking, snowshoeing, backpacking, fishing, and birdwatching. Regardless of the season, there are plenty of opportunities to explore the trails, with a variety of distances to choose from. Snow cover in the winter allows for snowshoeing, expanding your access to certain areas that may be off-limits without snow. North and South Shattuck, Jeanstow, Knickerbocker, Townline, Horseshoe, and Plummer lakes provide opportunities for boating, canoeing, and kayaking. Fishing is also available in the many lakes within the Chippewa Moraine. The David R. Obey Ice Age Interpretive Center features high-quality exhibits that delve into glacial, cultural, and natural history. The center includes a larger room for group presentations, as well as indoor and outdoor seating areas where visitors can take in scenic views to the south and west. Picnic tables are conveniently placed outside the interpretive center, making it a great spot for visitors to reconnect with nature and enjoy quality family time. Hunting and trapping are allowed within the property during legal hunting and trapping seasons. Prior to hunting or trapping, individuals must obtain a property map that identifies the areas closed to these activities within the property.

DATE(S) VISITED ....

LODGING ....

WHO I WENT WITH ....

WILL I RETURN? YES / NO

□ SPRING □ SUMMER □ FALL □ WINTER

□ ☀ □ ☁ □ 🌦 □ 🌧 □ ❄

FEE(S) .... PARK HOURS .... TEMP:.........

RATING ☆ ☆ ☆ ☆ ☆

NOTES

COPPER CULTURE STATE PARK

COUNTY	ESTABLISHED	AREA (AC/HA)
OCONTO	1959	42 / 17

Copper Culture State Park is historically significant as the location of a prehistoric cemetery utilized by the Old Copper Complex people who inhabited the northern Midwest from approximately 4000 to 2000 BC. This site, originally overlooked, gained recognition in 1952 when a 13-year-old boy stumbled upon human remains while playing in an old quarry. Spanning 42 acres, the park is situated just west of Oconto, providing an opportunity for visitors to explore its grounds, including a scenic walk along the Oconto River. Additionally, a museum on-site offers a collection of artifacts and exhibits that shed light on the property's significance. One can embark on a pleasant hiking trail leading to the river, marked with informative signage detailing the historical importance of the area. Fishing from the river's shore is also an option. The park and museum operations are overseen by the Oconto County Historical Society, ensuring the maintenance and tranquility of the park. Visitors are advised to bring insect repellent to make their experience more enjoyable.

DATE(S) VISITED .... ☐ SPRING ☐ SUMMER ☐ FALL ☐ WINTER

LODGING .... ☐ ☀ ☐ ☁ ☐ 🌧 ☐ 🌫 ☐ ❄

WHO I WENT WITH .... FEE(S) .... PARK HOURS .... TEMP:........

WILL I RETURN? YES / NO   RATING ☆ ☆ ☆ ☆ ☆

NOTES

PASSPORT STAMPS

COPPER FALLS STATE PARK

COUNTY	ESTABLISHED	AREA (AC/HA)
ASHLAND	1929	3,068 / 1,242

Copper Falls State Park, renowned for its ancient lava flows, deep gorges, and breathtaking waterfalls, stands out as one of the most picturesque parks in Wisconsin. The addition of log buildings, constructed in the 1930s by the Civilian Conservation Corps, enhances the park's overall charm. Visitors to the park can engage in a range of outdoor activities, including camping, hiking, biking, picnicking, fishing, and swimming in Loon Lake. One standout attraction is the 1.7-mile Doughboy's Nature Trail, following the course of the Bad River, widely regarded as one of Wisconsin's finest hiking experiences. The park boasts a network of trails that spans 17 miles, including a segment of the North Country National Scenic Trail. These trails are designed to accommodate hikers, cyclists, cross-country skiers, and snowshoers. Copper Falls State Park also offers opportunities for winter camping and ice fishing on Loon Lake. Cyclists and hikers can explore two one-way mountain bike trails—the Vahterra Trail to the east of the Ballfield parking lot and the Takesson Trail to the south of North Campground—during snow-free seasons. Bicycling is restricted to designated bike trails and park roads. Swimmers can take advantage of a 300-foot sandy beach at Loon Lake, which features a paved pathway leading to the water's edge. While there are no lifeguards on duty, the beach provides a safe and enjoyable swimming experience. For those interested in exploring the waters, the park offers small carry-in boat access to Loon Lake for canoes and kayaks. Additionally, there are several other lakes within a 10-mile radius of the park that provide boat launch facilities and opportunities for larger watercraft. Copper Falls State Park provides two campgrounds characterized by shaded and wooded sites thoughtfully separated from high-traffic public areas. This layout offers campers a sense of seclusion and tranquility. Anglers will appreciate the park's prime location within an excellent fishing area, with numerous nearby lakes offering diverse sport fishing opportunities. Loon Lake itself is a hotspot for largemouth bass, northern pike, and panfish. A generously sized picnic area, extending over 5 acres along the banks of the Bad River, features multiple picnic tables and grills, a spacious log shelter, a concession stand, and a playground. It serves as the starting point for the Doughboys Nature Trail, leading to Copper and Brownstone Falls. During the designated Wisconsin state parks hunting and trapping time frame, hunting and trapping are allowed in the park's open areas, providing opportunities for those interested in these activities.

PASSPORT STAMPS

COULEE EXPERIMENTAL STATE FOREST

COUNTY	ESTABLISHED	AREA (AC/HA)
LA CROSSE	1960	2,944 / 1,191

The Coulee State Experimental Forest, a unique property in the state of Wisconsin, serves as a dedicated site for conducting long-term forest watershed research aimed at the development of effective land management practices. The name "Coulee" aptly characterizes the area, given its numerous deep ravines and gullies. The property is carefully managed to achieve a balance between forest production and providing a conducive environment for wildlife habitat. Additionally, it offers recreational opportunities for hunting, cross-country skiing, hiking, and horseback riding. Horseback riding is permitted within the forest except in designated Native Community Management Areas, on the ski trails when they are snow-covered, and on any trail during the spring when the ground is soft. When the ski trails are not covered by snow, they can be used for hiking. Primitive forest roads are open to various forms of recreation, such as snowshoeing, wildlife viewing, and nature study. The Coulee Experimental State Forest, located in La Crosse County, stands as one of the few extensive public upland forests in the region, making it an ideal location for hunting various species. Key game species available for hunting include deer, ruffed grouse, squirrels, turkeys, and rabbits.

DATE(S) VISITED .... ☐ SPRING ☐ SUMMER ☐ FALL ☐ WINTER

LODGING .... ☐ ☀ ☐ ☁ ☐ 🌧 ☐ ⛆ ☐ ❄

WHO I WENT WITH .... FEE(S) .... PARK HOURS .... TEMP:.........

WILL I RETURN? YES / NO   RATING ☆ ☆ ☆ ☆ ☆

NOTES

PASSPORT STAMPS

COUNCIL GROUNDS STATE PARK

COUNTY	ESTABLISHED	AREA (AC/HA)
LINCOLN	1938	509 / 206

Situated along the picturesque Wisconsin River in proximity to Native American encampments, Council Grounds State Park has become a beloved destination for water enthusiasts. The park offers a wide range of recreational activities, including opportunities for both family and group camping, access to forest trails, a beach, and a convenient fishing pier designed for accessibility. The park boasts a 217-foot-long beach, providing ample space for sunbathing and relaxation, with an adjacent picnic area. While the prime swimming season falls between mid-June and mid-August, it's important to note that there are no lifeguards on duty. In addition to swimming, Council Grounds State Park is known for its popularity among boaters and water-skiers. The park features a boat landing near the accessible fishing pier and beach, granting access to both Lake Alexander and the Wisconsin River. During the appropriate season, visitors can rent canoes and kayaks from the Friends of Council Grounds State Park. Camping options are available, including family and group campsites. The park also offers a sizable picnic area, which is conveniently located near the beach at Alexander Lake. Other picnic areas can be found near the Big Pines Nature Trail and the refuge building. An accessible fishing pier is situated on the northwest side of the park, close to the boat landing. Fishing enthusiasts can expect to find a variety of fish species in Lake Alexander, such as northern pike, walleye, smallmouth bass, muskies, yellow perch, bluegills, and black crappies. For those who enjoy hiking, several trails traverse different sections of the park, providing options for flat or gently rolling terrain. Additionally, the 2.5-mile main road within the park is a popular choice for walkers and joggers. Council Grounds State Park has a rich history, having transitioned from being a city park in Merrill to a state forest before achieving full state park status in 1978. The park's open areas are accessible for hunting and trapping within the designated time frame set by Wisconsin state parks. In the winter, visitors can enjoy cross-country skiing and snowshoeing within the park's grounds.

DATE(S) VISITED .... □ SPRING □ SUMMER □ FALL □ WINTER

LODGING .... □ ☼ □ ☁ □ 🌧 □ 🌫 □ ❄

WHO I WENT WITH .... FEE(S) .... PARK HOURS .... TEMP:.........

WILL I RETURN? YES / NO   RATING ☆ ☆ ☆ ☆ ☆

NOTES

CROSS PLAINS STATE PARK

COUNTY	ESTABLISHED	AREA (AC/HA)
DANE	1971	1,500 / 610

The Ice Age Complex at Cross Plains is a part of the National Ice Age Scientific Reserve, located just to the west of Madison near the village of Cross Plains. This area boasts an exceptional array of glacial landforms, a gorge sculpted by meltwater, and expansive vistas that encompass both driftless and glaciated terrains. For fishing enthusiasts, Shoveler's Sink is a prime spot, and it's situated on land owned by the U.S. Fish and Wildlife Service. It's worth noting that anglers who are 16 years of age and older are required to possess a valid Wisconsin fishing license. Visitors are welcome to explore federal, state, and county lands year-round, making it an ideal destination for hikers and walkers. There are hiking trails available on DNR lands located north of Old Sauk Pass Road, as well as on National Park Service lands. During the Wisconsin state parks hunting and trapping season, hunting and trapping activities are permitted in the open areas of the DNR land situated to the south and west of Old Sauk Pass Road. The park also offers opportunities for winter activities, such as cross-country skiing, snowshoeing, and hiking.

DATE(S) VISITED .... ☐ SPRING ☐ SUMMER ☐ FALL ☐ WINTER

LODGING .... ☐ ☀ ☐ ☁ ☐ 🌧 ☐ 🌫 ☐ ❄

WHO I WENT WITH .... FEE(S) .... PARK HOURS .... TEMP:.........

WILL I RETURN? YES / NO   RATING ☆ ☆ ☆ ☆ ☆

NOTES

PASSPORT STAMPS

DEVIL'S LAKE STATE PARK

COUNTY	ESTABLISHED	AREA (AC/HA)
SAUK	1911	10,200 / 4,100

Devil's Lake State Park, situated along the Ice Age National Scenic Trail, provides breathtaking views from its 500-foot quartzite bluffs that overlook the 360-acre lake. The park offers a wide range of outdoor recreational opportunities for visitors to enjoy throughout the year. Guests can explore nearly 30 miles of hiking trails, relax in lakeside picnic areas, swim at the beaches, engage in paddling activities, and participate in year-round nature programs. The park features 1.5 miles of accessible trails for individuals with disabilities. These trails are not maintained for winter use but remain open. In addition to traditional winter activities like skiing and snowshoeing, visitors can also enjoy dog sledding, building igloos, geocaching, and orienteering courses. For biking enthusiasts, the park offers four miles of off-road bike trails, specifically the Upland Trail Loop. There are two free boat launches available within the park: one located on the north shore near the castle and the other along Park Road between the north and south shores. Devil's Lake State Park boasts two beaches, one at each end of the lake, totaling 3,300 feet in length. Each beach is equipped with a bathhouse, although no lifeguards are on duty. Scuba diving is a popular activity at the park, with required diving flags. Anglers frequent the park for lakeshore and boat fishing (electric motor only). The lake is home to a variety of fish species, including brook trout, walleye, northern pike, bass, and panfish. Ice fishing is also a favored pastime in winter, where anglers can catch brown trout, northern pike, and other fish. Devil's Lake State Park offers ample picnic areas on both the north and south shores, featuring tables, drinking water (in season), and grills for visitors to use. The park provides three regular campgrounds with a total of 423 sites for families ranging from one to six people. Additionally, there are nine group campsites available to accommodate up to 240 people, and all campgrounds are open for reservations. The park is known for its impressive quartzite rock formations, including iconic landmarks such as Balanced Rock and Devil's Doorway. During the Wisconsin state parks hunting and trapping season, hunting and trapping activities are allowed in the open areas of the park.

DATE(S) VISITED .... ☐ SPRING ☐ SUMMER ☐ FALL ☐ WINTER

LODGING .... ☐☀ ☐☁ ☐🌧 ☐🌦 ☐❄

WHO I WENT WITH .... FEE(S) .... PARK HOURS .... TEMP:.........

WILL I RETURN? YES / NO RATING ☆ ☆ ☆ ☆ ☆

NOTES

PASSPORT STAMPS

FISCHER CREEK STATE RECREATION AREA

COUNTY	ESTABLISHED	AREA (AC/HA)
MANITOWOC	1991	142 / 57

Fischer Creek boasts approximately one mile of shoreline along Lake Michigan, offering picturesque wooded bluffs, meadows, and wetlands. This location is an ideal spot for hiking, picnicking, observing wildlife, and unwinding on the beach. The area encompasses a blend of young forest, marshes, and grasslands, traversed by Fischer Creek, a Class II trout stream that experiences spring and fall fish runs from Lake Michigan. It is a serene and tranquil destination, providing visitors with an opportunity to relax and enjoy the natural surroundings. Fischer Creek features two parking lots, situated on either side of Fischer Creek itself.

DATE(S) VISITED .... □ SPRING □ SUMMER □ FALL □ WINTER

LODGING .... □ ☼ □ ☁ □ 🌧 □ 🌫 □ ❄

WHO I WENT WITH .... FEE(S) .... PARK HOURS .... TEMP:.........

WILL I RETURN? YES / NO RATING ☆ ☆ ☆ ☆ ☆

NOTES

PASSPORT STAMPS

FLAMBEAU RIVER STATE FOREST

COUNTY	ESTABLISHED	AREA (AC/HA)
SAWYER, PRICE	1930	90,147 / 36,481

The Flambeau River State Forest offers a wide range of outdoor opportunities, including forested hiking trails, ATV and snowmobile trails, family campgrounds, primitive riverside camping, hunting, and fishing. Canoeing is a particularly popular activity in the forest, with various parts of the Flambeau River offering different levels of difficulty for paddlers. The North Fork is well-suited for beginners, while the South Fork presents challenges for more experienced canoeists. The forest predominantly consists of northern hardwoods. For off-road enthusiasts, the Flambeau River State Forest provides 38 miles of ATV trails, typically open from May 15 to November 15. When using ATVs in the forest, it's essential to stay on designated trails. During the summer, cyclists can also enjoy the 14-mile Flambeau Hills Ski trail. The forest features two family campgrounds with reservable sites, and there are numerous access points to forest lakes and the Flambeau River for fishing, primarily through boat launches and fishing piers. Hiking enthusiasts will find several opportunities within the forest, including nature trails at Connors Lake Campground and Lake of the Pines Campground. Additionally, hiking is allowed on the Flambeau Hills Ski Trail during the summer and in winter when the trails aren't groomed for cross-country skiing. For those interested in hunting, the national forests in the area offer excellent conditions. Picnic facilities with amenities such as drinking water, flush toilets, picnic tables, grills, and playground equipment can be found at Connors Lake along W Highway.

DATE(S) VISITED ....   ☐ SPRING   ☐ SUMMER   ☐ FALL   ☐ WINTER

LODGING ....   ☐ ☀ ☐ ☁ ☐ 🌧 ☐ ⛈ ☐ ❄

WHO I WENT WITH ....   FEE(S) .... PARK HOURS .... TEMP:.........

WILL I RETURN? YES / NO   RATING ☆ ☆ ☆ ☆ ☆

NOTES

PASSPORT STAMPS

GOVERNOR DODGE STATE PARK

COUNTY	ESTABLISHED	AREA (AC/HA)
IOWA	1948	5,350 / 2,130

Governor Dodge State Park is situated in the scenic driftless area of Wisconsin, featuring rugged terrain with steep hills, bluffs, deep valleys, two lakes, and a picturesque waterfall. This park provides a wide range of outdoor activities for visitors to enjoy, including camping, picnicking, hiking, canoeing, biking, hunting, fishing, off-road biking, cross-country skiing, and horseback riding. Additionally, visitors can partake in boating and swimming in the park's two lakes. Named in honor of Henry Dodge, the first governor of the Wisconsin Territory, the park showcases geological features typical of the Driftless Area. In its natural setting, you can encounter a variety of wildlife species, including white-tailed deer, shrews, wild turkey, black grouse, beavers, red foxes, and gray foxes. For mountain biking enthusiasts, there are eight miles of challenging off-road bike trails within the park, with a State Trail Pass required for trail usage. Both Cox Hollow and Twin Valley lakes offer swimming beaches, and launch ramps are available for boating. Paddleboats and kayaks can be rented at the Cox Hollow Beach concession stand during the summer season and on select weekends in spring and fall. Anglers can take advantage of the excellent fishing opportunities in the park's lakes, with various species like bass, walleye, muskie, and panfish to be found. Fishing licenses are mandatory and can be obtained from local bait shops. Governor Dodge State Park offers over 300 campsites, including standard, group, equestrian, and remote backpacking sites. The park also maintains a network of approximately 40 miles of trails, accessible for hikers, except for the ski trails when covered in snow. Equestrian riders can explore 22 miles of bridle trails, providing a unique perspective of the park's diverse landscape. During the designated Wisconsin state parks hunting and trapping seasons, hunting and trapping activities are allowed in open areas of the park. Additionally, there are eight designated picnic sites, and picnic shelters can be found at various locations within the park, including Enee Point, the amphitheater, Twin Valley Picnic Area, and Cox Hollow and Twin Valley beaches.

DATE(S) VISITED .... ☐ SPRING ☐ SUMMER ☐ FALL ☐ WINTER

LODGING .... ☐ ☀ ☐ ☁ ☐ 🌧 ☐ ⛈ ☐ ❄

WHO I WENT WITH .... FEE(S) .... PARK HOURS .... TEMP:.........

WILL I RETURN? YES / NO   RATING ☆ ☆ ☆ ☆ ☆

NOTES

PASSPORT STAMPS

GOVERNOR EARL PESHTIGO RIVER STATE FOREST

COUNTY	ESTABLISHED	AREA (AC/HA)
MARINETTE	2001	12,400 / 5,018

The Governor Earl Peshtigo River State Forest, located along the Peshtigo River and adjacent to Governor Thompson State Park, is a long and narrow state forest in the northeast region of Wisconsin. It borders some of the most picturesque and thrilling segments of the Peshtigo River. Anglers are drawn to the free-flowing section of the river, renowned for its exceptional fly-fishing opportunities. Adventurous paddlers take on the Midwest's longest continuous whitewater rapids on this river. Within the Governor Earl Peshtigo River State Forest, there are over 3,200 acres of water, providing beautiful settings for boating and paddling. This expansive area includes access to the islands and backwaters of the Peshtigo River. Visitors to the state forest can enjoy two beaches. Old Veteran's Lake Beach features 10 acres of remarkably clear water and a small beach area for recreational purposes. For those looking to stay overnight, the forest offers a family campground and several remote boat-in campsites situated along the riverbanks. Additionally, a segment of the Woodland ATV Trail passes through the state forest, serving as the only area accessible to ATVs within the forest. In addition to the snowmobile trails that ATVs can use in the winter, this trail system offers another avenue for ATV enthusiasts. The national forest has two trail systems and features various roads and volunteer-maintained hiking trails that are suitable for hunters. While there are no specific equestrian trails or mountain bike trails designated in the state forest, these activities are generally permitted throughout the forest. Horseback riders and mountain bikers can utilize snowmobile trails and angler access roads except during the winter months. The Governor Earl Peshtigo River State Forest presents numerous opportunities for hunters and trappers who seek a variety of game. The majority of the forest's lands are open to hunting during the scheduled seasons, with primary game species including white-tailed deer, small game, black bear, and migratory birds. Trappers can find beaver, muskrat, raccoon, fisher, and mink in the area.

DATE(S) VISITED .... ☐ SPRING ☐ SUMMER ☐ FALL ☐ WINTER

LODGING .... ☐ ☀ ☐ ☁ ☐ 🌧 ☐ 🌩 ☐ ❄

WHO I WENT WITH .... FEE(S) .... PARK HOURS .... TEMP:.........

WILL I RETURN? YES / NO   RATING ☆ ☆ ☆ ☆ ☆

NOTES

PASSPORT STAMPS

GOVERNOR KNOWLES STATE FOREST

COUNTY	ESTABLISHED	AREA (AC/HA)
BURNETT, POLK	1970	19,753 / 7,993

The state forest's eastern boundary is defined by county forests and two state wildlife areas. Initially named the St. Croix River State Forest, it was officially renamed in 1981 to pay tribute to former Wisconsin governor Warren P. Knowles, in recognition of his strong commitment to conservation and his passion for the outdoors. This 55-mile-long forest, located in northwestern Wisconsin, runs parallel to the St. Croix National Scenic Riverway and offers a wide range of outdoor activities, including camping, paddling, hiking, horseback riding, biking, hunting, fishing, cross-country skiing, and snowmobiling. The forest's trail system is accessible for bicycles, with the exception of any trails that are specifically marked as closed. These trails are unpaved and off-road, offering various levels of difficulty. Within Governor Knowles State Forest, there are nine primitive campsites positioned along the hiking trails, providing opportunities for outdoor enthusiasts to connect with nature. For those interested in water activities, the Wood River can be canoed or kayaked from Grantsburg to Raspberry Landing on the St. Croix River. The St. Croix River meanders through a picturesque and untamed landscape, originating in the spruce-fir swamps near Upper St. Croix Lake. Governor Knowles State Forest boasts an extensive network of hiking trails, totaling 40 miles in length, which wind through the breathtaking St. John River valley. This trail system is divided into two segments, with the northern segment covering 23 miles and the southern segment spanning 17 miles. Hunters can take advantage of the forest's diverse wildlife, pursuing game such as deer, turkey, black bear, squirrels, grouse, and woodcock during the hunting seasons.

DATE(S) VISITED .... ☐ SPRING ☐ SUMMER ☐ FALL ☐ WINTER

LODGING .... ☐ ☀ ☐ ☁ ☐ 🌧 ☐ 🌫 ☐ ☁

WHO I WENT WITH .... FEE(S) .... PARK HOURS .... TEMP:.........

WILL I RETURN? YES / NO RATING ☆ ☆ ☆ ☆ ☆

NOTES

PASSPORT STAMPS

GOVERNOR NELSON STATE PARK

COUNTY	ESTABLISHED	AREA (AC/HA)
DANE	1975	422 / 171

Governor Nelson State Park was dedicated to pay tribute to the former Governor of Wisconsin, Gaylord Nelson. This day-use park offers a wide range of amenities and outdoor activities for visitors to enjoy. It features a sandy beach, a boat launch, facilities for cleaning fish, picnic areas with playground equipment, prairie restorations, and an extensive network of trails, covering over 8 miles. Aside from the lakeshore, visitors can explore various natural features within the park, such as restored prairies and savannas, Native American effigy mounds, hiking trails, and ski trails. The Woodland Trail, in particular, provides a glimpse of Native American effigy mounds. Governor Nelson State Park also boasts a four-stall boat launch, allowing easy access to Lake Mendota, which is home to a wide variety of game fish and panfish, making it an excellent spot for fishing throughout the year. For those looking to enjoy the natural beauty and ecological diversity of the park, there are 8.4 miles of hiking trails that wind through oak woodlands, savannas, and other ecosystems. The trails are adorned with vibrant wildflowers, and hikers often have the chance to spot various animals during their journey. Additionally, the park features two accessible viewing platforms along the trails, each equipped with informative boards. While picnicking in the park is possible with the provided grills, open campfires are not allowed. Governor Nelson State Park offers two shelters available for reservation, one located on the beach and the other in the picnic area. During the winter season, the park grooms its trails for cross-country skiing, providing options for both skiers who enjoy sloping terrain and those who prefer flatter, more moderate paths.

DATE(S) VISITED .... ☐ SPRING ☐ SUMMER ☐ FALL ☐ WINTER

LODGING .... ☐ ☀ ☐ ☁ ☐ 🌧 ☐ ☁ ☐ ❄

WHO I WENT WITH .... FEE(S) .... PARK HOURS .... TEMP:.........

WILL I RETURN? YES / NO   RATING ☆ ☆ ☆ ☆ ☆

NOTES

PASSPORT STAMPS

GOVERNOR THOMPSON STATE PARK

COUNTY	ESTABLISHED	AREA (AC/HA)
MARINETTE	2000	2,800 / 1,100

Governor Thompson State Park, located near Crivitz, Wisconsin, is a picturesque forested area with a prime location. The park boasts 6.5 miles of shoreline along the Caldron Falls Reservoir, which is a segment of the Peshtigo River, as well as 5,300 feet of shoreline along two small kettle lakes. The park shares boundaries with the Peshtigo River State Forest, enhancing the natural beauty and recreational opportunities in the region. Governor Thompson State Park provides a network of over 16 miles of hiking trails that allow visitors to explore the lush wilderness. While hiking, it's common to spot various wildlife, including black grouse, turkeys, white-tailed deer, and more. These trails can be enjoyed year-round, making the park an excellent destination for winter enthusiasts who can take advantage of the maintained cross-country skiing trail. For those who love water activities, the park offers a popular boat launch site on the Caldron Falls Reservoir, South Bay, commonly referred to as Boat Landing #13. This launch area is equipped with two concrete launches, a boarding dock, a fishing pier, a paved parking lot, a picnic area, and restroom facilities. Woods Lake, one of the small kettle lakes in the park, features a 150-foot sandy beach for swimming, along with a grassy sunbathing area and restroom facilities with changing areas. Governor Thompson State Park also offers a family campground and three boat sites for those who wish to spend extended periods in this natural oasis. Fishing opportunities abound, with the chance to catch bluegills, crappies, northern pike, and bass being particularly popular. Picnic tables and benches can be found in the Woods Lake area, creating an inviting atmosphere for visitors. Governor Thompson State Park accommodates hunting and trapping in open areas, aligning with the scheduled hunting and trapping seasons established by Wisconsin state parks. In the winter, the park's trails are groomed for both diagonal skiers and skate skiers, allowing for excellent cross-country skiing experiences.

PASSPORT STAMPS

HARRINGTON BEACH STATE PARK

COUNTY	ESTABLISHED	AREA (AC/HA)
OZAUKEE	1966	715 / 258

Harrington Beach State Park, situated along Lake Michigan, boasts over a mile of pristine beachfront. The park's natural features include a white cedar and hardwood swamp, open fields with restored wetland ponds, and a picturesque limestone quarry lake. It offers a range of outdoor activities, making it a versatile destination for visitors. Activities at Harrington Beach State Park include camping, sunbathing, picnicking, hiking, birdwatching, fishing, and even astronomy. The park hosts monthly public viewings at its observatory, providing a unique opportunity for stargazing. The park's history is intertwined with the operation of a dolomite quarry that spanned from the 1890s to 1925. The Quarry Lake Trail at Harrington Beach State Park is wheelchair accessible, ensuring that all visitors can enjoy the park's natural beauty. Biking is allowed on the shuttle bus route that runs from the Puckett's Pond area to the Ansay Welcome Center. While there is no boat launch within the park, those using small watercraft should be mindful of Lake Michigan's wind conditions. Swimming and boating are not allowed in Quarry Lake or Puckett's Pond. Accommodation options at Harrington Beach State Park include a family campground, which features five walk-in sites, a group campsite, an accessible cabin for individuals with disabilities, and a designated kayak site. The park is well-known for surf fishing, attracting anglers in pursuit of salmon and trout along the shores of Lake Michigan. Additionally, fishing opportunities can be found at the 26-acre Quarry Lake and Puckett's Pond, where species like trout, crappie, bluegill, and others can be caught. With seven miles of hiking trails, Harrington Beach State Park provides plenty of opportunities for scenic walks. As you stroll along Lake Michigan's shoreline, you can even spot the remnants of a historic 700-foot pier that was once used for shipping limestone quarried and processed within the park. This pier is located at the point where the north and south beaches meet. There are also beautiful picnic areas within the park, offering fantastic views of Lake Michigan. Reservation shelters are available at these areas, as well as at the Puckett's Pond picnic spot near the upper parking lot. Sand volleyball courts are also provided within the park. Hunting and trapping are permitted in the open areas of the park in accordance with the designated hunting and trapping seasons established by Wisconsin state parks. In the winter, the park offers a cross-country ski trail that runs from the lower parking lot along the shuttle bus route to the Hardwood Swamp trail, then loops back east along the service road. A snowmobile trail runs through the west end of the park.

DATE(S) VISITED .... ☐ SPRING ☐ SUMMER ☐ FALL ☐ WINTER

LODGING .... ☐ ☀ ☐ ☁ ☐ 🌧 ☐ ⛆ ☐ ❄

WHO I WENT WITH .... FEE(S) .... PARK HOURS .... TEMP:.........

WILL I RETURN? YES / NO   RATING ☆ ☆ ☆ ☆ ☆

NOTES

PASSPORT STAMPS

HARTMAN CREEK STATE PARK

COUNTY	ESTABLISHED	AREA (AC/HA)
WAUPACA	1966	1,500 / 573

Nestled around the picturesque Chain O' Lakes, Hartman Creek State Park is a serene and cherished natural destination in central Wisconsin. The park is a haven for outdoor enthusiasts and offers a range of activities, including camping, boating, swimming, horseback riding, mountain biking, and the chance to explore the historic Hellestad House log cabin. It also provides visitors with picturesque picnic spots like Whispering Pines along Marl Lake. During the summer, the park truly shines, with seven pristine lakes featuring crystal clear waters, a sandy swimming beach, and an extensive network of diverse trails. Hikers can explore approximately 10 miles of trails within Hartman Creek State Park. Before becoming a state park in 1966, this area was a fish hatchery, where dams were constructed to create four spring-fed lakes: Allen, Hartman, Grebe, and Middle. The park is situated on a section of the terminal moraine left behind by the Wisconsin glacier, and the lakes are fed by natural features like potholes, gullies, and springs. Furthermore, the Ice Age National Scenic Trail traverses the park, offering additional opportunities for exploration. For mountain biking enthusiasts, the park boasts around 12 miles of off-road biking trails, many of which are shared hiking and biking segments. Hartman Lake features a 300-foot sandy beach along with a spacious designated swimming area. Adjacent to the beach is a three-acre multi-use lawn area that includes picnic tables, drinking water, and combined changing and restroom facilities. Paddlers can set out on their canoes or kayaks from the boat landing located off Knight Lane on Manomin Lake. They can paddle through the eastern section of Hartman Creek State Park, including the Pope Lake Natural Area, en route to Marl Lake. At Marl Lake's floating dock, a stone staircase leads to the Whispering Pines picnic area, providing a great place for paddlers to pause for lunch. The picnic area is well-equipped with tables, grills, restrooms, drinking water, and vehicle access, with a parking lot accessible via Whispering Pines Road. Hartman Creek State Park features a family campground with 103 campsites and five group camping sites. The park's lakes are teeming with largemouth bass, perch, bluegill, and other panfish, making it a hotspot for fishing. Fishing piers, designed to be accessible to individuals with disabilities, can be found along the eastern shore of Allen Lake and at Whispering Pines on Marl Lake. The park offers four distinct picnic areas equipped with tables, benches, grills, drinking water, and parking facilities. In accordance with the Wisconsin state parks hunting and trapping time frame, hunting and trapping are permitted in open areas of the park. Hartman Creek State Park is a well-rounded destination for those who appreciate the beauty of the outdoors and offers a diverse array of recreational activities for all to enjoy.

DATE(S) VISITED .... ☐ SPRING ☐ SUMMER ☐ FALL ☐ WINTER

LODGING .... ☐ ☀ ☐ ☁ ☐ 🌧 ☐ ⛅ ☐ ❄

WHO I WENT WITH .... FEE(S) .... PARK HOURS .... TEMP:.........

WILL I RETURN? YES / NO   RATING ☆ ☆ ☆ ☆ ☆

NOTES

PASSPORT STAMPS

HAVENWOODS STATE FOREST

COUNTY	ESTABLISHED	AREA (AC/HA)
MILWAUKEE	1979	237 / 95,9

Havenwoods State Forest was established with the primary goal of offering an urban green space and serving as an environmental education center. This expansive area encompasses diverse landscapes, including grasslands, woodlands, wetlands, Lincoln Creek, an urban arboretum, and educational gardens. The Environmental Awareness Center, a hub of learning and engagement, features an auditorium, classrooms, informative displays, and a resource center. For those seeking outdoor experiences, Havenwoods provides a network of trails suitable for nature study, hiking, biking, and cross-country skiing. Schoenecker Park shares a boundary with the forest, particularly to the northeast. Cyclists can explore the forest's limestone trails and paved roads covering approximately 2 miles, but it's important to exercise caution as these trails are shared with pedestrians. The forest offers more than 6 miles of trails that cater to hikers, runners, and joggers, allowing them to venture through woodlands, wetlands, and meadows. With various sections of trails, visitors can choose routes of different lengths based on their preferences. Those who wish to enjoy a meal outdoors can have a picnic anywhere within the forest, with designated picnic tables available in the Urban Arboretum and near the parking lot. However, open fires or barbecues are not permitted. Winter enthusiasts, especially cross-country skiers, are welcomed to explore the forest during the colder months. It's worth noting that the trails are not groomed, making the terrain at Havenwoods generally flat and suitable for beginners looking for a pleasant cross-country skiing experience.

DATE(S) VISITED ....

LODGING ....

WHO I WENT WITH ....

WILL I RETURN? YES / NO

☐ SPRING ☐ SUMMER ☐ FALL ☐ WINTER

☐ ☀ ☐ ☁ ☐ 🌧 ☐ 🌫 ☐ ❄

FEE(S) .... PARK HOURS .... TEMP:.........

RATING ☆ ☆ ☆ ☆ ☆

NOTES

PASSPORT STAMPS

PASSPORT STAMPS

HERITAGE HILL STATE PARK

COUNTY	ESTABLISHED	AREA (AC/HA)
BROWN	1973	48 / 19

Heritage Hill State Park is home to a remarkable collection of 26 historic and reproduction structures, many of which are endangered historic buildings that were relocated from various places. These structures encompass a range of architectural styles and time periods, including log cabins dating back to the fur trade era, buildings from Fort Howard, and stores and public buildings from the late 19th century. Previously, this land served as a prison farm, and it was managed by inmates who maintained orchards. The construction of a new bridge over the Fox River led to the isolation of the farm from the prison, resulting in the land's transfer to the State of Wisconsin Department of Natural Resources. Within Heritage Hill State Park, visitors can explore more than 6,600 artifacts, with the majority of them thoughtfully displayed within the various buildings. This remarkable collection includes original artwork, books, clothing, and furnishings that span from the 17th century to the present day, offering valuable insights into the region's history and heritage.

DATE(S) VISITED .... ☐ SPRING   ☐ SUMMER   ☐ FALL   ☐ WINTER

LODGING .... ☐ ☀ ☐ ☁ ☐ 🌧 ☐ 🌥 ☐ ❄

WHO I WENT WITH .... FEE(S) .... PARK HOURS .... TEMP:.........

WILL I RETURN? YES / NO   RATING ☆ ☆ ☆ ☆ ☆

NOTES

PASSPORT STAMPS

HIGH CLIFF STATE PARK

COUNTY	ESTABLISHED	AREA (AC/HA)
CALUMET	1954	1,147 / 464

High Cliff State Park derives its name from the prominent cliffs of the Niagara Escarpment, a geological formation situated east of Lake Winnebago's shore. This escarpment stretches northward through northeastern Wisconsin, Upper Michigan, and Ontario, ultimately leading to Niagara Falls in New York State. One of the park's notable features is a majestic 12-foot statue of Winnebago Indian Chief Red Bird, positioned atop a massive granite rock, providing a captivating vantage point overlooking Lake Winnebago. High Cliff State Park offers a range of outdoor recreational activities, including camping, picnicking, boating, swimming, fishing, and hunting. The park boasts a variety of hiking trails, with options like the 6-mile limestone-surfaced Indian Mound Trail. These hiking trails cater to varying levels of difficulty and are designed as looped paths of differing lengths. At the pinnacle of the escarpment, visitors can take in picturesque views of Lake Winnebago from a 40-foot-tall observation tower. High Cliff provides various trails for activities such as biking, horseback riding, cross-country skiing, snowshoeing, and snowmobiling. Bicycles are permitted on all park roads, and designated trails for cyclists include the Bike/Horse Trail and the Red Bird Trail. The park boasts 8.5 miles of horse trails, though horse rentals are not available on-site. High Cliff State Park features four developed boat launches, offering easy access to Lake Winnebago for water enthusiasts, including windsurfers, kiteboarders, and paddleboarders. A state park admission sticker is a requisite for using these launches. The park also offers a swimming area, though it's essential to note that there are no lifeguards on duty. The bathhouse provides amenities like flush toilets, showers, changing rooms, and open shelters. For those interested in camping, High Cliff State Park offers multiple options, including family camping, an outdoor group camp, and a cabin designed to accommodate people with disabilities. The family campground encompasses 112 campsites, with 32 of them featuring electric hookups, and two are handicap accessible. Additionally, there are eight group campsites available. Anglers have opportunities for fishing in both Butterfly Pond and Lake Winnebago. The pond is known to yield largemouth bass and panfish, while the lake offers prospects for catching walleye, white bass, and perch. Archery hunting and trapping are permissible in the open areas of the park during the designated Wisconsin state parks hunting and trapping season. High Cliff State Park is equipped with four picnic areas, each furnished with tables, grills, water access, and restrooms. Two of these areas also feature playgrounds and swings for recreational enjoyment. Finally, during the winter months when snow blankets the landscape, specific trails in the park are designated for skiing. These trails are groomed to accommodate traditional skiing styles, making them suitable for both novice and intermediate skiers.

DATE(S) VISITED ....   ☐ SPRING   ☐ SUMMER   ☐ FALL   ☐ WINTER

LODGING ....   ☐ ☀   ☐ ☁   ☐ 🌧   ☐ ⛅   ☐ ☂

WHO I WENT WITH ....   FEE(S) ....   PARK HOURS ....   TEMP:.........

WILL I RETURN? YES / NO   RATING ☆ ☆ ☆ ☆ ☆

_____
_____
_____
_____
_____
_____
_____
_____
_____
_____
_____
_____
_____
_____
_____
_____
_____
_____
_____
_____
_____
_____
_____
_____
_____
_____
_____
_____
_____
_____
_____
_____
_____
_____

PASSPORT STAMPS

HOFFMAN HILLS STATE RECREATION AREA

COUNTY	ESTABLISHED	AREA (AC/HA)
DUNN	1980	707 / 286

Hoffman Hills boasts an extensive network of hiking trails, encompassing more than nine miles of pathways, including two miles dedicated to nature trails. These trails offer the opportunity to explore a 15-acre tallgrass prairie preserve or engage in wildlife observation along a handicap-accessible one-mile trail traversing a wetland. It's essential to note that these trails are reserved for hiking only, and no bicycles, motorized vehicles, or horses are permitted. For visitors seeking breathtaking panoramic views, a prominent 60-foot observation tower is available, providing spectacular vistas of the surrounding landscape. Three designated picnic areas within Hoffman Hills offer ideal spots for outdoor dining and relaxation. It's worth noting that the area is accessible for the nine-day gun deer season in November but remains closed during all other hunting or trapping seasons. During the winter season, Hoffman Hills presents a winter wonderland with its nine miles of ski trails. These trails cater to a range of skill levels and are meticulously groomed to accommodate both skate and step skiing. Importantly, the groomed ski trails are reserved for skiing and are not intended for activities such as sledding, snowboarding, snowshoeing, or regular hiking.

DATE(S) VISITED .... ☐ SPRING ☐ SUMMER ☐ FALL ☐ WINTER

LODGING .... ☐ ☀ ☐ ☁ ☐ 🌧 ☐ 🌫 ☐ ❄

WHO I WENT WITH .... FEE(S) .... PARK HOURS .... TEMP:.........

WILL I RETURN? YES / NO   RATING ☆ ☆ ☆ ☆ ☆

NOTES

PASSPORT STAMPS

INTERSTATE STATE PARK

COUNTY	ESTABLISHED	AREA (AC/HA)
POLK	1900	1,330 / 540

Interstate State Park holds the distinction of being the oldest state park in Wisconsin. Nestled along the picturesque St. Croix National Scenic Riverway, this park offers stunning vistas of the river and is home to a dramatic gorge known as the Dalles of the St. Croix. Visitors to the park can delve into Wisconsin's glacial history at the Ice Age Interpretive Center, where they can explore exhibits featuring films, photos, murals, and informative displays. Outdoor enthusiasts have a range of activities to choose from, including scaling the cliffs of the St. Croix Dalles River, leisurely canoeing down the calm waters, witnessing kayakers navigate the rushing rapids, or simply enjoying a serene tour boat ride. Canoe rentals are conveniently available outside the park's boundaries. Lake O' the Dalles boasts a sandy beach area along with a beach house, although it's essential to note that there are no lifeguards present. Spring in the park brings forth a diverse array of wildflowers, adding a touch of natural beauty. The geological landscape of the park is equally intriguing, with more than ten distinct lava flows exposed, coupled with two prominent glacial deposits and remnants of ancient streams, valleys, and faults. Summer presents an ideal time for hiking the park's trails and exploring the unique glacial sinkholes that define the park's character. Over nine miles of hiking trails await exploration, offering numerous opportunities to savor the park's breathtaking scenery and natural features. Guided hikes are also available during the summer months, adding an educational dimension to your visit. The hiking trails vary in difficulty, catering to a range of skill levels. Interstate Park is a sought-after destination for camping, offering two campgrounds and a primitive group camp for visitors to choose from. Several designated areas within the park are equipped with picnic tables, fireplaces, grills, water access, and restroom facilities. For those planning group outings, the park also provides picnic shelters that can be reserved in advance. In the winter season, Interstate Park transforms into a haven for outdoor recreation, with approximately 12.5 miles of trails catering to cross-country skiing, snowshoeing, and hiking. The St. Croix River running through the park is renowned for its excellent fishing opportunities, supporting a variety of game fish, including walleyes, northern pike, muskies, and small-mouth bass. During the established Wisconsin state parks hunting and trapping timeframe, these activities are permitted in the open areas of the park.

DATE(S) VISITED ....

☐ SPRING   ☐ SUMMER   ☐ FALL   ☐ WINTER

LODGING ....

☐ ☼   ☐ ☁   ☐ ☂   ☐ ☃   ☐ ❄

WHO I WENT WITH ....

FEE(S) .... PARK HOURS .... TEMP:.........

WILL I RETURN? YES / NO

RATING ☆ ☆ ☆ ☆ ☆

NOTES

PASSPORT STAMPS

KETTLE MORAINE STATE FOREST

COUNTY	ESTABLISHED	AREA (AC/HA)
WASHINGTON	1937	22,000 / 8,903

Spanning over 22,000 acres of forested glacial terrain, lakes, and prairies, the South Branch of the Kettle Moraine State Forest offers a diverse natural landscape with a network of more than 100 miles of trails, catering to various outdoor activities such as mountain biking, horseback riding, hiking, and nature exploration. Visitors can also engage in rowing, sailing, swimming, fishing, hunting, and winter sports within the forest's boundaries. With a vast trail system spanning 30 miles, the South Branch of the Kettle Moraine State Forest presents a haven for off-road biking, accommodating everyone from novice riders to seasoned enthusiasts. Hiking enthusiasts can traverse several trails in the forest, including the Scuppernong, Emma Carlin, John Muir, and Nordic trails, as well as the Ice Age National Scenic Trail. Additionally, there are several shorter self-guided nature trails for those interested in more leisurely walks. In the winter months, the Nordic and McMiller trails provide opportunities for cross-country skiing when snow conditions permit. Camping, paddling, boating, swimming, fishing, and hunting round out the array of activities offered within the forest. The southern region of the Kettle Moraine National Forest boasts two swimming beaches, situated at Lake Ottawa and Lake Whitewater. It's important to note that these beaches do not have lifeguards, and visitors are expected to adhere to the "carry in, carry out" rule, meaning that they should take their trash with them upon departure. Picnic areas with tables, grills, and restroom facilities are conveniently located near the beaches. For group gatherings and activities, the Southern Unit of the Kettle Moraine State Forest provides picnic tables, grills, and shelters at various recreation areas and trails. Additionally, an amphitheater at one location is available for reservations. Boat launches are situated within the forest at Ottawa Lake, Rice Lake, and Whitewater Lake, facilitating easy access to aquatic activities. There are four lakes within or in close proximity to the southern unit of the Kettle Moraine State Forest, ranging in size from 28 to 640 acres, with a combined area of 860 acres. These lakes are inhabited by a variety of fish species, including panfish and walleye, along with muskellunge, largemouth and smallmouth bass, trout, and northern pike. For anglers with disabilities, Ottawa Lake features an accessible fishing pier, and Whitewater Lake provides two handicap-accessible fishing stations. Most of the Southern Unit of the Kettle Moraine State Forest, which encompasses approximately 22,000 acres, is open to hunting during established hunting seasons.

NOTES

PASSPORT STAMPS

KINNICKINNIC STATE PARK

COUNTY	ESTABLISHED	AREA (AC/HA)
PIERCE	1972	1,239 / 501

This park is situated at the confluence of the Kinnickinnic River and the St. Croix River. The point where the Kinnickinnic River flows into the St. Croix River forms a sandy delta, providing a scenic spot for boaters to enjoy picnicking and camping. The area is a hub for various water activities, with swimming, water skiing, sunbathing, and windsurfing being particularly popular. The banks of the Kinnickinnic River are lush with Weymouth pines, creating a picturesque backdrop for visitors. On the St. Croix River, there's a designated sandy swimming area, marked with buoys for safety. Anglers can indulge in fishing on the St. Croix River, which is renowned for its large walleye population but also offers a wide range of other fish species. The Kinnickinnic River, a designated trout stream, boasts a thriving population of German brown trout. Nature enthusiasts can explore approximately 10 miles of hiking trails within the park. In the northern section of the park, the trails are reasonably well marked, with colored tape on posts at major intersections. Visitors can also find maps at many of these intersections if needed. Off-road biking is restricted to the Red Trail specifically. Throughout the park, there are various picnic areas equipped with tables and grills, making it convenient for visitors to enjoy outdoor meals. The most expansive picnic area can be found at the St. Croix viewpoint, while another popular spot for picnicking is near the swimming area. In the winter months, cross-country ski trails are available for those eager to partake in this activity. Additionally, hunting and trapping are permitted in the open areas of the park, following the established Wisconsin state parks hunting and trapping schedules.

DATE(S) VISITED .... ☐ SPRING ☐ SUMMER ☐ FALL ☐ WINTER

LODGING .... ☐ ☀ ☐ ☁ ☐ 🌧 ☐ ⛈ ☐ ❄

WHO I WENT WITH .... FEE(S) .... PARK HOURS .... TEMP:.........

WILL I RETURN? YES / NO   RATING ☆ ☆ ☆ ☆ ☆

NOTES

PASSPORT STAMPS

PASSPORT STAMPS

KOHLER-ANDRAE STATE PARK

COUNTY	ESTABLISHED	AREA (AC/HA)
SHEBOYGAN	1928	988 / 400

Kohler-Andrae State Park is comprised of two adjoining state parks situated in the city of Wilson, Wisconsin. These parks offer more than 2 miles of picturesque beaches and dunes along the shoreline of Lake Michigan. A range of Lake Michigan activities is available, including fishing, boating, and swimming. The lake is home to numerous fish species, such as trout and salmon, providing ample opportunities for fishing. Visitors can also enjoy fishing in the accessible fishing pond located on Old Park Road. Inland activities at Kohler-Andrae State Park encompass hiking and biking. The park boasts two nature trails and three hiking trails, offering visitors various options to explore the natural beauty of the area. Whether you prefer a leisurely walk along the nature trails, a trek through the dune cordons, or a stroll along the Lake Michigan shoreline, the park has plenty of hiking opportunities to choose from. Bicycles are permitted on all park roads, and off-road bicycling is allowed on the Black River Trail. Additionally, the Black River Trail welcomes horseback riders. While the park doesn't have a boat launch, individuals with small watercraft should be mindful of the prevailing wind conditions on Lake Michigan. Swimming in Lake Michigan is permitted, but it's essential to exercise caution as there are no lifeguards on duty. Kohler-Andrae State Park offers various accommodation options, including a family campground, group campground, and an accessible cabin designed for individuals with disabilities. Additionally, the park features both open and enclosed shelters as well as an amphitheater, all available for reservations. During the established Wisconsin state parks hunting and trapping seasons, hunting and trapping are permitted in the park's open areas. In the winter, cross-country skiing is a popular activity, with a marked one-mile trail and a two-mile ski trail featuring flat or gently sloping terrain. The longer trail runs through a variety of beautiful settings, starting at the picnic area and passing through the wooded south campground.

DATE(S) VISITED .... □ SPRING □ SUMMER □ FALL □ WINTER

LODGING .... □☀ □☁ □🌧 □🌩 □❄

WHO I WENT WITH .... FEE(S) .... PARK HOURS .... TEMP:.........

WILL I RETURN? YES / NO   RATING ☆ ☆ ☆ ☆ ☆

NOTES

PASSPORT STAMPS

LAKE KEGONSA STATE PARK

COUNTY	ESTABLISHED	AREA (AC/HA)
DANE	1962	343 / 139

Lake Kegonsa State Park offers a wide range of recreational activities for visitors to enjoy. The park provides opportunities for swimming, fishing, water skiing, boating, and features a convenient boat landing. Access to the lake is possible via various watercraft, including boats, canoes, kayaks, sailboats, and other personal watercraft. The park includes a designated swimming beach on Kegonsa Lake, complete with a nearby bathhouse. It's important to note that there are no lifeguards on duty at the beach, and pets are not allowed in this area. The fishing opportunities in Kegonsa Lake are excellent, and the park boasts hiking trails that wind their way through diverse landscapes, including oak woodlands, prairies, and wetlands. Lake Kegonsa State Park is well-regarded for its campground, beach, and a network of hiking trails that covers approximately 5 miles. Kegonsa Lake itself is a natural wonder, with a depth exceeding 30 feet. This lake was formed by the glacial activity during the last ice age, which took place around 12,000 years ago. Thanks to its unique features and aquatic ecosystems, Kegonsa Lake is a fantastic location for year-round fishing. Local vendors offer boat rentals and live bait, ensuring that visitors have the necessary resources for a successful fishing trip. It's important to note that a valid fishing license is required for all anglers. Kegonsa Lake is particularly renowned for its diverse fish species and the quality of fishing opportunities it presents. The lake is well-known for its walleye and panfish populations, making it a favorite among fishing enthusiasts. Lake Kegonsa State Park provides both family and group campgrounds, which are open for visitors from May 1 through October 31. The park also offers five picnic sites and two reservation picnic shelters, each equipped with a volleyball court and horseshoe pit nearby. In the winter, cross-country skiing is a popular activity in the park. Approximately five miles of trails, including the 1.2-mile White Oak nature trail, are groomed and tracked when snow and weather conditions permit. These trails are prepared for diagonal-stride skiers and are also groomed for skate skiing. Additionally, during the established Wisconsin state parks hunting and trapping seasons, archery hunting and trapping are allowed in the park's open areas, with the exception of gun hunting, which is not permitted.

PASSPORT STAMPS

LAKE WISSOTA STATE PARK

COUNTY	ESTABLISHED	AREA (AC/HA)
CHIPPEWA	1962	1,062 / 430

Lake Wissota State Park provides a wide range of outdoor activities and amenities for visitors to enjoy. The park features campsites, a variety of hiking and biking trails, opportunities for horseback riding, as well as picnic and playground areas. Additionally, a swimming beach is available on a man-made lake within the park. During the summer, the lake is a hub for various water activities, including sailing, kayaking, and water skiing, making it a popular spot for outdoor enthusiasts. To facilitate easy access to the lake, Lake Wissota State Park offers a boat landing and a trailer park on the south side of the park. Visitors can also rent kayaks from the Friends of Lake Wissota State Park at the park office, where a list of local businesses that offer fishing boat rentals is also available. Lake Wissota is home to several fish species, such as walleyes, muskies, bass, panfish, northern pike, catfish, and sturgeon, providing ample opportunities for fishing. Please note that a valid Wisconsin fishing license is required. Additionally, there is a permanent accessible fishing pier situated along the shore just west of the boat launch. The park's landscape comprises a diverse mix of pine and hardwood forests, as well as prairie areas. Nature enthusiasts can access the Old Abe State Trail, a 20-mile hiking and biking trail leading to Brunet Island State Park. Biking is a popular activity at Lake Wissota State Park, with a majority of the park's terrain being flat. Over 11 miles of park trails are open to off-road biking. For horseback riding enthusiasts, there are nine miles of designated trails within the park, with horseback riders aged 16 and older requiring a state trail pass for access. Lake Wissota State Park offers camping options for both families and groups. Birdwatchers will appreciate the park's significance as more than 200 species of birds pass through the area during spring and fall migrations. Birdwatchers can obtain species checklists from the park office. For picnicking, the park provides four picnic shelters, two of which are available for rent. There are picnic areas situated along the lake near the beach and fishing pier. A spacious playground can be found at the family campground, and the park features amenities like a soccer field and a volleyball court. During established Wisconsin state parks hunting and trapping seasons, these activities are allowed in the open areas of the park. In the winter months, visitors can enjoy approximately eight miles of groomed cross-country ski trails catering to both traditional stride and skate skiing. The park also maintains about 10 miles of open trails for snowshoeing.

NOTES

PASSPORT STAMPS

LAKESHORE STATE PARK

COUNTY	ESTABLISHED	AREA (AC/HA)
MILWAUKEE	1998	22 / 8,9

The park serves as an urban sanctuary featuring a small beach and wheelchair-accessible paved trails that link to other Lake Michigan parks in Milwaukee and the Hank Aaron State Trail. Situated amid scenic views of the city and Lake Michigan, the park boasts a boat landing for which overnight reservations can be made. With water encompassing the majority of its boundaries, Lakeshore State Park is connected to Urban Park through the picturesque Lakeshore State Park bridge. Visitors can partake in fishing activities, and running paths traverse the park's grounds. Fishing is permissible anywhere along the Lakeshore shoreline, excluding the pedestrian bridge. For those interested in fishing, an accessible fishing pier is available on the south lagoon, accessible via the west trail on the island. The park's lagoons also offer excellent opportunities for kayaking, with kayaks launchable and landable on the beach or via the stone steps at the island's south end. In the winter, the park remains open for hiking and snowshoeing. Birdwatching is a prevalent activity, allowing enthusiasts to observe various northern waterfowl up close as they frequent the park's lagoons. However, hunting and trapping are not permitted on the property.

DATE(S) VISITED .... ☐ SPRING ☐ SUMMER ☐ FALL ☐ WINTER

LODGING .... ☐☀ ☐☁ ☐🌧 ☐🌫 ☐❄

WHO I WENT WITH .... FEE(S) .... PARK HOURS .... TEMP:.........

WILL I RETURN? YES / NO   RATING ☆ ☆ ☆ ☆ ☆

NOTES

PASSPORT STAMPS

LOST DAUPHIN STATE PARK

COUNTY	ESTABLISHED	AREA (AC/HA)
BROWN	1947	19 / 7,7

Lost Dauphin State Park is situated adjacent to the Fox River, positioned slightly to the south of the town of De Pere. The park is renowned for its hiking trails and pleasant picnicking spots. This area was once inhabited by Eleazer Williams, a historical figure who claimed to be connected to the Lost Dauphin. His residency in the mid-19th century has left a lasting imprint on the landscape. The park features a picturesque vantage point overlooking the Fox River, equipped with a bench, shelter, and swings to enhance visitors' experiences. Additionally, the site preserves the flagstone foundation of the former house, serving as a historical testament to the past. Lost Dauphin State Park is under the local management of the Town of Lawrence.

DATE(S) VISITED .... ☐ SPRING ☐ SUMMER ☐ FALL ☐ WINTER

LODGING .... ☐ ☀ ☐ ☁ ☐ 🌧 ☐ 🌫 ☐ ❄

WHO I WENT WITH .... FEE(S) .... PARK HOURS .... TEMP:.........

WILL I RETURN? YES / NO   RATING ☆ ☆ ☆ ☆ ☆

NOTES

PASSPORT STAMPS

LOWER WISCONSIN STATE RIVERWAY

COUNTY	ESTABLISHED	AREA (AC/HA)
GRANT, BOUNDARY, DANE	1989	45,000 / 18,211

The Lower Wisconsin State Riverway is a picturesque location close to urban areas, offering various outdoor activities like fishing, hunting, canoeing, boating, hiking, and horseback riding. You can also take in the river's scenic views while driving on country roads. The area is rich in bird and wildlife populations, with canoes being the preferred mode of transportation. Most river trail users are concentrated between Prairie du Sac and Spring Green. For a more secluded experience, the section from Spring Green to Boscobel is ideal, and the stretch below Boscobel offers the utmost solitude. The Wisconsin River Valley is characterized by impressive bluffs, forested valleys, and sandy shores, featuring numerous islands for camping and outdoor recreation minus the crowds. Camping options are available on islands, sandbars, two state parks (Wyalusing and Tower Hill), and several private and municipal campgrounds. Wyalusing and Tower Hill state parks, both situated along the river, provide boat launch facilities, with family campgrounds at Wyalusing and a smaller one at Tower Hill, all of which can be reserved. State-owned islands and sandbars allow camping for a maximum of three days, and campers must carry out their trash. Hiking trails are located at Ferry Bluff and Black Hawk Ridge. Black Hawk Ridge offers diverse terrain and a historic battle site to explore, with a rewarding panoramic view of the Wisconsin River Valley after a short but steep hike up Ferry Bluff, where an informative exhibit awaits at the trail's end. Mountain bikes are prohibited on these trails, except for fat-tire bikes in winter. All-terrain vehicles (ATVs) and other off-road vehicles are not allowed on the River Trail. Additionally, the riverway offers approximately 20 miles of horseback riding trails at Black Hawk Ridge and Millville, offering stunning vistas as they traverse the ridges above the river valley.

DATE(S) VISITED ....   ☐ SPRING ☐ SUMMER ☐ FALL ☐ WINTER

LODGING ....   ☐ ☀ ☐ ☁ ☐ ☁ ☐ ☁ ☐ ☁

WHO I WENT WITH ....   FEE(S) .... PARK HOURS .... TEMP:.........

WILL I RETURN? YES / NO   RATING ☆ ☆ ☆ ☆ ☆

NOTES

PASSPORT STAMPS

PASSPORT STAMPS

MACKENZIE CENTER

COUNTY	ESTABLISHED	AREA (AC/HA)
COLUMBIA	1930	280 / 113,3

The MacKenzie Center offers educational trails, displays, museums, and educational programs tailored for school groups and youth. It's a fantastic destination to explore and gain knowledge about the natural world. The logging museum, situated in a log home constructed in the early 1880s near Grantsburg, houses visual materials showcasing Wisconsin's late 19th-century logging industry, historical tools utilized for timber harvesting, and two dioramas illustrating logging practices. Adjacent to the logging museum, a sawmill exhibit allows visitors to observe the lumber processing methods from the early days of Wisconsin's booming lumber trade. You can also discover the process of making sugar and maple syrup here. MacKenzie Center features several self-guided nature trails. These trails commence at the wildlife area entrance, wind through the woods, and connect with the logging museum. At the property's southern end, about half a mile from the main parking area, there's a trail system that comprises five nature trails, one of which is wheelchair accessible. It's important to note that the MacKenzie Center is not open for hunting during public hunting seasons, but it does host various Learn to Hunt events throughout the year. For visitors looking to enjoy a meal outdoors, the MacKenzie Center provides a grassy picnic area with a shelter that can be reserved. This shelter is positioned on a lawn next to a wooded area, offering ample parking, picnic tables, grills, and nearby flush toilets. Reservations can be made for the shelter.

DATE(S) VISITED .... ☐ SPRING ☐ SUMMER ☐ FALL ☐ WINTER

LODGING .... ☐ ☀ ☐ ☁ ☐ 🌧 ☐ 🌨 ☐ ❄

WHO I WENT WITH .... FEE(S) .... PARK HOURS .... TEMP:.........

WILL I RETURN? YES / NO   RATING ☆ ☆ ☆ ☆ ☆

NOTES

PASSPORT STAMPS

MENOMINEE RIVER STATE RECREATION AREA

COUNTY	ESTABLISHED	AREA (AC/HA)
MARINETTE	2010	7,652 / 3,096

This area stretches along the scenic Menominee River in northeastern Wisconsin for several miles. Visitors have the opportunity to paddle along the river, passing through tall pine forests, rock formations, and waterfalls, or they can explore this serene location for primitive camping, hiking, fishing, and hunting. It's a picturesque spot for wildlife enthusiasts, offering campsites and boat access points along the river. The property includes a simple canoe landing at Quiver Falls, a concrete boat landing at Saler Landing on Rattie Road, and a gravel boat landing in Pemene on Horseshoe Road. There are additional marinas on the Michigan side of the river and off the farm. Most of the river is wide and calm, with some occasional rapids. A mandatory portage is required on the Michigan side at Pemene Falls. The Menominee River is well-known for smallmouth bass fishing, and it also supports various other fish species. Hikers can explore the Pemene Falls Trail in the Pemene Falls unit or the Sand Portage hiking trail in the Piers Gorge unit. There are other trails and logging roads on the property, although they aren't officially maintained or managed as designated trails. The property allows hunting and trapping during the legal hunting and trapping seasons and offers opportunities for snowshoeing and ungroomed cross-country skiing. Additionally, Marinette County ATV/snowmobile trails pass through certain sections of the property.

DATE(S) VISITED .... ☐ SPRING ☐ SUMMER ☐ FALL ☐ WINTER

LODGING .... ☐☼ ☐☁ ☐🌧 ☐🌨 ☐❄

WHO I WENT WITH .... FEE(S) .... PARK HOURS .... TEMP:.........

WILL I RETURN? YES / NO   RATING ☆ ☆ ☆ ☆ ☆

NOTES

PASSPORT STAMPS

MERRICK STATE PARK

COUNTY	ESTABLISHED	AREA (AC/HA)
BUFFALO	1932	320 / 130

Merrick State Park is situated on the picturesque floodplains of the Mississippi River, offering a wide range of year-round recreational activities. The park features a variety of campgrounds, some of which provide direct access to the river for mooring watercraft or fishing right from the campsites. With 65 individual campsites spread across three campgrounds and a group tents-only campsite accommodating up to 50 people, the park caters to campers of all kinds. Registered campers can even moor boats overnight at each campground. Hiking enthusiasts can explore the park's 2-mile network of hiking trails, which link various areas and offer relatively easy hiking suitable for people of all ages. Along the Mississippi River, you'll find picnic areas equipped with tables, access to fishing spots, wildlife viewing opportunities, and a chance to unwind and enjoy the scenery. Additionally, one of the picnic areas near the lower boat launch allows leashed pets. For those interested in water-based activities, the Mississippi River teems with large and smallmouth bass, bluegills, crappies, and more. Merrick State Park boasts two boat launches that can accommodate most motorized boats, with ample parking at both marinas. Kayakers can conveniently access the water via a canoe landing near the lower marina, making it an ideal spot for a serene paddle through the quiet backwaters. The park even offers a self-guided canoe trail that starts and ends near the lower boat landing, with markers to guide your way. During the winter months, cross-country skiing is a popular pastime in Merrick. The park's trail system and undeveloped areas covered in natural snow are perfect for skiers who prefer off-trail adventures. Hunting and trapping are permitted in the park's open areas, following Wisconsin State Parks hunting and trapping regulations.

DATE(S) VISITED .... ☐ SPRING ☐ SUMMER ☐ FALL ☐ WINTER

LODGING .... ☐ ☀ ☐ ☁ ☐ 🌧 ☐ 🌨 ☐ ❄

WHO I WENT WITH .... FEE(S) .... PARK HOURS .... TEMP:.........

WILL I RETURN? YES / NO   RATING ☆ ☆ ☆ ☆ ☆

NOTES

PASSPORT STAMPS

MILL BLUFF STATE PARK

COUNTY	ESTABLISHED	AREA (AC/HA)
MONROE, JUNEAU	1936	1,337 / 541

Mill Bluff State Park, a part of the Ice Age National Scientific Reserve, offers breathtaking views of unique rock formations. This park safeguards a collection of striking sandstone bluffs, standing anywhere from 80 to 200 feet tall, which originated as sea stacks around 12,000 years ago in Glacial Lake Wisconsin. Consequently, these bluffs possess steep, angular features that set them apart from the more rounded landscapes found in the eastern United States. Located just outside Camp Douglas, the park features campsites, picnic areas, a shelter, hiking trails, and a swimming pond. The park's rustic family campground comprises 21 sites and is open from late May through September. Additionally, there are two picnic areas in Mill Bluff, situated on the east and west sides of Funnel Road. Each area is equipped with a shelter, picnic tables, grills, water sources, restrooms, and parking facilities. Visitors can enjoy a 2.5-acre pond with clear, cool water sourced from underground springs and a 250-foot white sand beach, providing a lovely spot for public swimming. While there are no biking trails within the park, the nearby Omaha Bike Trail in Juneau County, spanning 15 miles, can be reached from the park via County Highway W and County Highway C, leading into Camp Douglas. The Omaha bike trail also connects to the Elroy-Sparta State Trail and the 400 State Trail in Elroy. Mill Bluff boasts over two miles of hiking trails that offer panoramic vistas of the park's mesas, buttes, and pinnacles. Stairways lead to the summit of Mill Bluff. Note that pets are not allowed on the nature trail or within the picnic and swimming areas. Although Mill Bluff State Park lacks on-site staffing during the winter, it remains open for visitors. Many people take advantage of the marked trails for hiking, snowshoeing, or cross-country skiing, even though the trails are not groomed or maintained for winter use. Hunting and trapping are permitted in the open sections of the park, following Wisconsin State Parks hunting and trapping regulations. Small game and deer hunting are allowed in the park.

DATE(S) VISITED .... ☐ SPRING ☐ SUMMER ☐ FALL ☐ WINTER

LODGING .... ☐ ☀ ☐ ☁ ☐ 🌧 ☐ 🌫 ☐ ❄

WHO I WENT WITH .... FEE(S) .... PARK HOURS .... TEMP:.........

WILL I RETURN? YES / NO   RATING ☆ ☆ ☆ ☆ ☆

NOTES

PASSPORT STAMPS

MIRROR LAKE STATE PARK

COUNTY	ESTABLISHED	AREA (AC/HA)
SAUK	1962	2,192 / 882

Mirror Lake State Park provides a wide range of recreational activities for people of all ages. During the summer, visitors can rent boats, canoes, and kayaks from the park's concession stand. There are about 9 miles of trails available for off-road cycling enthusiasts, which are open from May 1 to October 31 each year, depending on weather and conditions. These trails are not accessible to bicycles, including fat-tire bikes, between November 1 and April 30 due to cross-country skiing and trail maintenance. These trails include the Hastings, Fern Dell, Turtleville, and Wild Rice Trails and are situated on the south side of Fern Dell Road. For those interested in additional biking options, the 400 State Trail is a 15-minute drive from Mirror Lake State Park in Reedsburg. Mirror Lake boasts two boat landings, one within the state park that also offers concessions and boat rentals, and the other is the Delton town launch located on Lakeview Road off State Highway 23 at the west end of the lake. The park includes a swimming beach with nearby restroom facilities, though it's important to note that there are no lifeguards on duty, and pets are not permitted on the beach. The entire lake operates under a slow-no-wake rule. Camping options at Mirror Lake State Park include 151 family camping sites spread across three separate campgrounds, as well as seven group sites. These campsites are primarily wooded, featuring beautiful pine and oak trees as the dominant forest cover. Each campsite comes equipped with a fire pit and picnic table, with most sites also having a sandy camping area. Fishing opportunities are available in both Mirror Lake and Dell Creek. Dell Creek, a 10.5-mile waterway that flows into Mirror Lake, provides cool water and suitable hiding spots for trout, though it relies on stocking as there is no natural spawning gravel. Nature enthusiasts can explore over 19 miles of hiking trails within Mirror Lake State Park. There are three separate picnic sites in the park, each with an accessible picnic shelter that can be reserved. Additionally, the large picnic area surrounding the swimming beach is equipped with picnic tables and grills. During the winter months, Mirror Lake State Park offers a variety of recreational opportunities, including groomed trails for cross-country skiing, snowshoeing, and hiking, as well as winter camping and ice fishing. The park also permits hunting and trapping in open areas, following Wisconsin State Parks hunting and trapping regulations.

NATURAL BRIDGE STATE PARK

COUNTY	ESTABLISHED	AREA (AC/HA)
SAUK	1972	530 / 210

Natural Bridge State Park offers diverse outdoor recreational opportunities year-round, but it's designated for day use only. The park boasts a remarkable natural sandstone arch that was sculpted by the erosive forces of wind and water. This arch has dimensions of 25 feet in height and 35 feet in width. Interestingly, this unique formation escaped the attention of the glaciers during the last Ice Age. Near the natural bridge, there's a rock shelter that served as a refuge for indigenous people approximately 11,000 years ago when the glacier was in retreat. The park's landscape is characterized by hills covered with oak and other hardwood trees, and certain ridge tops feature small prairie remnants with various grasses and cacti. Visitors can explore roughly 4 miles of hiking trails in Natural Bridge, all of which start at the spacious parking area on County Highway C. One of these trails is a nature trail that provides information on the traditional use of native plants by Native Americans. South of the highway, a 2-mile hiking trail winds through the woods. Climbing the natural arch or entering the shelter is not allowed, as these areas are preserved to protect the park's natural environment. The park's predominant natural land cover consists of oak woodland, complemented by open fields and patches of native prairie. Many wildflowers bloom throughout the growing season, and birdwatchers might spot various avian species, including vultures, woodpeckers, and bald eagles during the winter months. Natural Bridge State Park also features a large picnic area with tables next to the parking lot on County Highway C. In the winter, cross-country skiing is permitted within the park, even though there are no groomed ski trails. Winter hiking and snowshoeing are also welcomed throughout the park. Additionally, hunting and trapping are allowed in the open areas of the park, following Wisconsin State Parks hunting and trapping regulations.

DATE(S) VISITED .... □ SPRING □ SUMMER □ FALL □ WINTER

LODGING .... □ ☼ □ ☁ □ 🌧 □ ☁ □ ❄

WHO I WENT WITH .... FEE(S) .... PARK HOURS .... TEMP:.........

WILL I RETURN? YES / NO   RATING ☆ ☆ ☆ ☆ ☆

NOTES

PASSPORT STAMPS

NELSON DEWEY STATE PARK

COUNTY	ESTABLISHED	AREA (AC/HA)
GRANT	1935	756 / 306

Nelson Dewey State Park offers a commanding view of the Mississippi River from a 500-foot bluff. This land was once part of the Stonefield estate, owned by Nelson Dewey, Wisconsin's inaugural governor. The park presents visitors with a network of hiking trails, encompassing over two miles in total. These trails vary in difficulty, with five of them measuring less than a mile in length, yet providing a range of scenic experiences. Numerous trails within the park afford excellent vistas of the Mississippi River Valley. Notably, the park is home to the Dewey House and the nearby Stonefield Historic Site. Guests can partake in a variety of outdoor activities, ranging from engaging park programs to birdwatching and wildlife observation at Dewey Heights Prairie. Nelson Dewey State Park accommodates campers, including individuals, families, and small and large groups. For supplies and groceries, as well as laundry facilities, you can find them in Cassville, which is situated approximately 2 miles south of the park. It's worth noting that the park itself doesn't offer direct river access, but there is a boat landing in the city of Cassville at Riverside Park. Additionally, if you're looking to fish, Riverside Park in Cassville is a popular spot for anglers. Within Nelson Dewey State Park, there are three designated picnic areas: Mound Point, Dewey Heights, and Cedar Point. Each of these areas is equipped with picnic tables and grills for your convenience. The Dewey Heights picnic area stands out with two handicap-accessible picnic shelters and restrooms that are also handicap-accessible. During the winter season, visitors can explore the park's trails on foot, by skiing, or with snowshoes. For those interested in hunting and trapping, these activities are allowed in the open areas of the park, in accordance with Wisconsin State Parks hunting and trapping regulations.

DATE(S) VISITED .... ☐ SPRING ☐ SUMMER ☐ FALL ☐ WINTER

LODGING .... ☐ ☀ ☐ ☁ ☐ 🌧 ☐ 🌨 ☐ ❄

WHO I WENT WITH .... FEE(S) .... PARK HOURS .... TEMP:.........

WILL I RETURN? YES / NO   RATING ☆ ☆ ☆ ☆ ☆

NOTES

PASSPORT STAMPS

NEW GLARUS WOODS STATE PARK

COUNTY	ESTABLISHED	AREA (AC/HA)
GREEN	1934	435 / 175

The park encompasses a landscape of rolling hills that are a mix of forested areas and prairies. It's conveniently connected to the Sugar River State Trail, providing access to the park by bicycle. This trail also links up with the Badger State Trail. New Glarus Woods State Park offers camping and picnic facilities. During the summer, the park provides more than 24 miles of hiking trails, inviting exploration of the undulating terrain and observation of various wildlife, including deer, squirrels, turkeys, a variety of songbirds, and woodpeckers. Anglers can also enjoy fishing in the many streams that meander through the park. Bicycles are permitted on all paved surfaces within the park and campgrounds. New Glarus Woods State Park features both family and group campsites. The family campgrounds offer 18 drive-in campsites suitable for tent, pop-up, and small recreational vehicle camping, along with 14 "walk-to" sites for tent camping. Additionally, the park provides a spacious picnic area equipped with cooking grills, picnic tables, a large playground, an open-air picnic shelter with lights and electricity, vault toilet restrooms, and drinking fountains. A smaller picnic area with grills and tables is located near the walk-to campsites. It's important to note that bicycles are not permitted on hiking trails. The Sugar River Trail Spur passes through the campground and links to the 24-mile Sugar River State Trail. For those in need of bike rentals, they are available in the village of New Glarus at the Sugar River State Trailhead. In the winter, visitors can take pleasure in cross-country skiing and snowshoeing within the park. Furthermore, hunting and trapping are permitted in the open areas of the park, adhering to Wisconsin State Parks hunting and trapping regulations.

DATE(S) VISITED .... □ SPRING □ SUMMER □ FALL □ WINTER

LODGING .... □ ☼ □ ☁ □ 🌧 □ 🌫 □ ❄

WHO I WENT WITH .... FEE(S) .... PARK HOURS .... TEMP:........

WILL I RETURN? YES / NO   RATING ☆ ☆ ☆ ☆ ☆

NOTES

NEWPORT STATE PARK

COUNTY	ESTABLISHED	AREA (AC/HA)
DOOR	1964	2,373 / 960

This park is situated near the Lake Michigan shoreline and boasts an extensive network of over 30 hiking trails. It offers a wide range of outdoor activities, including hiking, swimming, fishing, backpacking, skiing, and snowshoeing. The park's landscape comprises evergreen and deciduous forests, wetlands, and upland meadows. It is home to an interpretive center and offers nature programs. Notably, Newport State Park is recognized for its exceptionally dark skies, making it one of the finest places for night sky observation. It's a prime destination for astronomy enthusiasts and stargazers alike. Nestled at the far end of the Door Peninsula along the shores of Lake Michigan, Newport State Park stands out as one of the darkest locations in the state, providing an opportunity to experience the true depth of a dark, natural sky. It has been designated as a Dark Sky Park by the International Dark-Sky Association, one of just 18 in the United States and the second in the Midwest. The park features bike trails primarily consisting of hard-packed dirt. These trails are generally considered easy to moderate, featuring no significant changes in elevation. Hiking is also permitted on all bike trails, and approximately 17 miles of the trails are open to off-road bicycles. It's important to note that there is no boat launch within the park, so users of small watercraft should be mindful of wind conditions on Lake Michigan. For campers, Newport State Park offers rustic backpack camping, and camping is allowed exclusively in designated campgrounds. A picnic area with a shelter is available on Newport Bay, situated near parking lot #3, and you can reserve any available shelters in the picnic area. Fishing opportunities are abundant in both Lake Michigan and Lake Europe in the northern region of the park. During the winter months, the park provides more than 26 miles of trails for cross-country skiing, including 12 miles of groomed trails for Nordic skiing and 2 miles for skate skiing. Snowshoeing is also welcomed, with about 5 miles of trails open for this activity. Lastly, hunting and trapping are allowed in the open areas of the park, adhering to Wisconsin State Parks hunting and trapping regulations.

DATE(S) VISITED .... ☐ SPRING ☐ SUMMER ☐ FALL ☐ WINTER

LODGING .... ☐ ☀ ☐ ☁ ☐ 🌦 ☐ ⛆ ☐ ❄

WHO I WENT WITH .... FEE(S) .... PARK HOURS .... TEMP:.........

WILL I RETURN? YES / NO   RATING ☆ ☆ ☆ ☆ ☆

NOTES

NORTHERN HIGHLAND AMERICAN LEGION STATE FOREST

COUNTY	ESTABLISHED	AREA (AC/HA)
VILAS, ONEIDA, IRON	1925	236,000 / 95,506

The forest provides a wide array of outdoor recreational activities, including camping, hiking, biking, snowmobiling, boating, fishing, hunting, and bird watching. Beyond recreation, the forest is also a hub for research programs. The presence of lakes, streams, and rivers offers hundreds of miles of waterways for exploration by canoe or kayak, with some water bodies accommodating motorized boats. The forest boasts an impressive biodiversity, home to 224 species of birds, which amounts to nearly three-quarters of the bird species found in the state of Wisconsin. It's important to note that All-Terrain Vehicles (ATVs) are strictly prohibited throughout the Northern Highland American Legion State Forest, except for the nature trails, Fallison, Trout Lake, Star Lake, and Raven's yellow loop. Biking is generally allowed on all roads and trails, except for designated mountain bike trails, which require a state trail pass. These passes can be obtained through self-registration at the trailheads. Specifically designated biking trails within the forest include McNaughton, Madeline, Lumberjack, and Raven. The forest is in close proximity to two trails suitable for all bike types: the Bearskin State Trail, with trailheads in Minocqua and near Highway 51, and a paved bike trail maintained by surrounding towns that stretches from Boulder Junction, through Crystal, Firefly, Muskie, North Trout, and South Trout campgrounds, ultimately leading to St. Germain. Camping options within the forest vary, ranging from modern to rustic, group, and primitive campsites. Some campgrounds are equipped with accessible facilities. The forest features seven hiking trails and four nature trails, and there are also numerous old logging roads, lesser-used town roads, logging roads, and snowmobile trails that offer excellent hiking opportunities. There are no designated riding trails within the state forest for equestrians; however, horses can be ridden in various areas, including public roads, old logging roads, and snowmobile trails (when not snow-covered). Horses are not allowed in campgrounds, on beaches, designated hiking trails, or nature trails. The Northern Highland American Legion State Forest is renowned for its vast network of lakes, making it the region with the highest concentration of lakes in Wisconsin. With over 900 lakes and more than 300 miles of rivers and streams, water recreation is a major draw for visitors. Additionally, the forest offers numerous picnic areas. During the winter, the forest provides four picturesque cross-country ski trails: Escanaba, Madeline, McNaughton, and Raven. Usage of these trails requires state passes, and since they are designated for cross-country skiing, they are off-limits for snowshoeing, hiking, and pets in the winter season. Hunting is also permitted within the forest, subject to Wisconsin State Parks hunting regulations.

DATE(S) VISITED .... □ SPRING □ SUMMER □ FALL □ WINTER

LODGING .... □ ☀ □ ☁ □ 🌧 □ ⛆ □ ❄

WHO I WENT WITH .... FEE(S) .... PARK HOURS .... TEMP:.........

WILL I RETURN? YES / NO   RATING ☆ ☆ ☆ ☆ ☆

NOTES

PASSPORT STAMPS

PATTISON STATE PARK

COUNTY	ESTABLISHED	AREA (AC/HA)
DOUGLAS	1920	1,400 / 566

Pattison State Park, situated on the Black River, boasts two remarkable waterfalls: the towering 165-foot Big Manitou Falls, the tallest waterfall in Wisconsin, and the diminutive 31-foot Little Manitou Falls, the smallest waterfall in the state. The park offers a wide array of activities centered around the Black River, including swimming, fishing, boating, and paddleboarding. However, recreational fishing opportunities within the park are somewhat limited. The lake does not support a sport fish population, and although there is occasional fishing in the Black River below Big Manitou Falls, the numbers have dwindled since the Department of Natural Resources (DNR) ceased stocking this area. For the latest information on fishing seasons, size limits, and fish populations, it's advisable to contact the park office. Pattison State Park also features a lake with a sandy beach, a nature center, a campground, and scenic hiking trails. The park boasts over 7 miles of hiking trails that follow the course of the Black River. Originating approximately 22 miles southwest of the park at Black Lake, near the Wisconsin-Minnesota border, the river winds its way through Pattison State Park, creating the 31-foot Little Manitou Falls, forming Interfalls Lake, and culminating in the awe-inspiring Big Manitou Falls. Hiking the trails along the Black River offers stunning views of the waterfalls. The park's campground provides 59 family camping sites and three backpacking sites. Additionally, there are three picnic areas equipped with tables, grills, water sources, and restrooms, with the largest one located near the beach. Playground equipment is available in the main picnic area. The park offers an enclosed building with a shelter at the primary picnic area, which can be rented for gatherings. Pattison State Park's Interfalls Lake boasts a 300-foot sandy beach, complete with excellent sunbathing spots, a well-appointed bathhouse, and an adjacent picnic area. It's important to note that the beach is not staffed by lifeguards, and swimming beyond the designated lifeline, in the river, or near the waterfalls is considered hazardous. For geology enthusiasts, the park is a fascinating destination with dark magma rocks scattered throughout the area. Visitors can even observe traces of earthquake and lava damage that occurred billions of years ago. The park's natural diversity is further highlighted by the presence of almost 200 bird species, 54 mammal species, and numerous reptiles and amphibians. In the winter, Pattison State Park offers 5.5 miles of classic cross-country ski trails. These trails vary in difficulty from beginner to moderate and start from the campground, consisting of three interconnected loops. Additionally, there are many informal trails in the park suitable for snowshoeing during the winter season. Lastly, hunting and trapping are allowed in the open areas of the park, in accordance with Wisconsin State Parks hunting and trapping regulations.

PENINSULA STATE PARK

COUNTY	ESTABLISHED	AREA (AC/HA)
DOOR	1909	3,776 / 1,528

Peninsula State Park is renowned for its towering bluffs, reaching heights of up to 150 feet, which provide breathtaking views from their summits. Many consider Peninsula State Park to be the most comprehensive and well-rounded park in Wisconsin, and a closer look at its wide array of offerings readily explains why. Starting from the Fish Creek entrance to the park, the Sunset Trail, featuring fine gravel and relatively flat terrain, is suitable for bicycles, wheelchairs, and hikers. The trail meanders through various landscapes, including Weborg Marsh, areas with cedar and maple trees, and cliff communities. The Sunset Bike Route, which connects to a return route at Nicolet Beach, extends for an additional four miles along the park's scenic back roads. For those traveling to and from Nicolet Bay, the Hidden Bluff offers a scenic 0.75-mile shortcut, granting access to the nature center. Nicolet Beach, located within the park, provides a swimming area (without lifeguards), as well as rentals of kayaks and other watercraft, a snack bar, and ample sandy shores for sunbathing. Exploring the peninsula from the water offers stunning vistas, excellent fishing opportunities, and plenty of fun. The park's eight-mile shoreline is a popular destination for power boaters, sailors, and kayakers, and a launch ramp can be found in Nicolet Bay. Day use parking is available for vehicles and trailers near the ramp. Campers on the peninsula have the option to park their trailers overnight in the parking lot near the amphitheater. Kayaks are frequently launched in Tennison Bay, which is conducive to shallow draft watercraft. Overnight anchoring is permitted in Horseshoe Island and in Nicolet Bay, outside the designated boating and launching area. Fishing enthusiasts will find Weborg Pier to be a prime location for catching smallmouth and rock bass, as well as brown trout. Peninsula State Park is considered Wisconsin's top camping destination, offering a total of 468 family campsites across its five campgrounds, along with three group sites for tent camping. Winter camping is available at Tennison Bay campground, which has designated campsites. Golf enthusiasts can take advantage of Peninsula State Park's 18-hole golf course and a six-hole learning Short Course. The park is also home to a network of hiking trails that spans a total of 20 miles. Numerous picnic areas are scattered throughout the Peninsula, including Fish Creek (near the park headquarters), Nelson Point, Nicolet Beach, Pines Area, Eagle Terrace, Weborg Point, and Welcker's Point. These areas are equipped with tables, charcoal grills, and restroom facilities. In the winter, Peninsula State Park offers 16 miles of groomed ski trails, most of which are double-tracked. Skaters can access six miles of trails groomed for both classical and skate skiing. Additionally, there are six miles of designated snowshoe and hiking trails during the winter months. Hunting and trapping are allowed in open areas of the park during the hunting and trapping season, in accordance with Wisconsin state park regulations.

DATE(S) VISITED .... ☐ SPRING ☐ SUMMER ☐ FALL ☐ WINTER

LODGING .... ☐ ☀ ☐ ☁ ☐ 🌧 ☐ 🌦 ☐ ❄

WHO I WENT WITH .... FEE(S) .... PARK HOURS .... TEMP:.........

WILL I RETURN? YES / NO   RATING ☆ ☆ ☆ ☆ ☆

NOTES

PASSPORT STAMPS

PERROT STATE PARK

COUNTY	ESTABLISHED	AREA (AC/HA)
TREMPEALEAU	1918	1,200 / 485

Perrot State Park spans 1,200 acres and is situated amidst 500-foot bluffs at the confluence of the Trempealeau and Mississippi rivers. The park is renowned for its stunning river vistas and is valued for its wealth of natural, archaeological, and historical assets. For cyclists, direct access is available from the campground to the 24-mile Great River State Trail. Additionally, there is a marked canoe trail in Trempealeau Bay, and canoes can be rented at the park during the season. Perrot State Park offers numerous family campsites and four walk-in group campsites. Campers can conveniently access the Great River State Trail from the campground. A boat landing on the Trempealeau River offers access to Trempealeau Bay and the Mississippi River via a railroad bridge. Fishing opportunities are available along the shore. However, it's important to note that the Trempealeau River's water level varies throughout the year and is relatively shallow within the park. Fishing in Trempealeau Bay can yield different results depending on the season and water levels. Nearby areas provide additional opportunities for shore fishing and boat access. There is also a boat landing in Trempealeau that connects to the Mississippi River. The Trempealeau Lakes Recreation Area offers shoreline fishing, an accessible fishing pier, and boat docks. Perrot State Park boasts 12.5 miles of hiking trails, many of which lead to the summits of the bluffs and offer unparalleled panoramic views of the Mississippi River Valley. The bluff trails can be steep, and some feature steps or stairs. To get a closer look at the river and Trempealeau Bay, you can hike the entire length of the park along the Riverview Trail. Throughout the park, there are six picnic areas located along the trails and near the nature center. These areas provide an ideal place to relax after a bluff hike, observe wildlife, or enjoy a beautiful sunset over Trempealeau Bay from below the nature center. Each picnic area is equipped with grills, and facilities, as well as water, are available during the season. There is a picnic shelter near the nature center that does not require reservations. Additionally, there are a volleyball net and horseshoe pits near the nature center, with horseshoes and volleyballs available for borrowing at the park headquarters. When weather conditions permit, nine miles of trails are groomed and tracked for cross-country skiing, with skate skiing permitted on a one-mile section within the campground. Groomed ski trails are off-limits to hikers, snowshoers, and pets. Hunting and trapping are permitted in open areas of the park, in accordance with Wisconsin State Parks hunting and trapping regulations.

NOTES

PASSPORT STAMPS

POINT BEACH STATE FOREST

COUNTY	ESTABLISHED	AREA (AC/HA)
MANITOWOC	1938	3,029 / 1,225

The forest provides a wide range of outdoor activities, including hiking, biking, swimming, picnicking, fishing, and boating. It boasts a network of 17 miles of hiking trails, with the longest one stretching over 7 miles. Point Beach offers two shelters, along with picnic areas near the shelter, allowing visitors to enjoy the picturesque views of Lake Michigan. Additionally, there are amenities like a playground, volleyball courts, and a baseball field. The picnic areas within Point Beach State Forest are fully equipped with picnic tables, outdoor grills, potable water, and restroom facilities. Point Beach State Forest features 127 camping sites, many of which come with electrical hookups, ensuring a comfortable camping experience. The forest also offers six miles of sandy beach along Lake Michigan, providing a serene environment for swimming in a woodland setting. It's important to note that there are no lifeguards on duty, and campfires are not permitted on the beach. A separate designated area is allocated for beachgoers with dogs. The forest does not provide a boat launching facility, so those with small watercraft or boating equipment should be mindful of Lake Michigan's varying wind conditions. In the vicinity, visitors can explore the Rawley Point Lighthouse, which has been under the operation and maintenance of the U.S. Coast Guard since 1853. Cyclists can enjoy well-maintained bike paths like the Ridges Trail, which includes three interconnected loops for off-road biking. The Rawley Point Bicycle Trail, starting at the lodge parking lot, takes riders through pine and hemlock forests for a scenic 5-mile route. This trail features a hard-packed limestone base and connects to the Mariners Trail, a 7-mile paved trail along the Lake Michigan shoreline leading to Two Rivers and Manitowoc. Another biking option is the Red Pine Trail, accessible from the parking lot west of County Highway O, opposite the forest entrance road. This 3.1-mile trail is open to both mountain bikers and hikers in the summer and to skiers during the winter season. Point Beach State Forest provides various winter activities with well-marked ski trails and opportunities for snowmobiling. Hunting and trapping are allowed on the property during the designated legal hunting and trapping seasons.

DATE(S) VISITED .... ☐ SPRING ☐ SUMMER ☐ FALL ☐ WINTER

LODGING .... ☐ ☼ ☐ ☁ ☐ 🌧 ☐ ⛆ ☐ ❄

WHO I WENT WITH .... FEE(S) .... PARK HOURS .... TEMP:.........

WILL I RETURN? YES / NO RATING ☆ ☆ ☆ ☆ ☆

NOTES

POTAWATOMI STATE PARK

COUNTY	ESTABLISHED	AREA (AC/HA)
DOOR	1928	1,200 / 485

The park derives its name from the Bo-De-Wad-Me tribe, which historically inhabited the Green Bay shores and surrounding islands when European settlers first arrived in the region. The name Bo-De-Wad-Me translates to "keeper of the fire." Potawatomi State Park boasts multiple hiking trails and serves as the eastern endpoint of the Ice Age National Scenic Trail. These park trails accommodate various activities, including hiking, biking, cross-country skiing, and snowmobiling. For cross-country skiing enthusiasts, the park offers four groomed trails, collectively spanning around 8.5 miles. Moreover, there are approximately eight miles of off-road biking paths throughout the park. Cyclists can find bicycle parking near the picnic areas along the shoreline at Parking Lot 1. It's worth noting that hikers are also permitted to ride bicycles on all park roads. Potawatomi State Park provides several picnic areas along the scenic Sturgeon Bay shoreline, as well as a viewpoint that overlooks the park's former ski hill. Playgrounds can be found within the picnic area at Parking Lot 2 and at the Daisy Field campground. Visitors have the option to reserve a shelter located in the picnic area along the park's southern shoreline, which features a fireplace and electrical outlets. The park offers family and group campsites, along with an accessible cabin designed for individuals with disabilities. Serving as a hub for water-based activities, Potawatomi State Park is ideal for boating, kayaking, canoeing, fishing, SCUBA diving, and water skiing on Green Bay. Over two miles of shoreline provide numerous scenic vistas and opportunities for outdoor recreation. The park encompasses a boat landing situated in Sawyer Harbor, a sheltered cove at the mouth of Sturgeon Bay. Visitors can rent canoes, kayaks, and paddleboats within the park, and there's a fish cleaning station at the boat launch. Anglers aged 16 years or older must possess a valid Wisconsin fishing license. Fishing equipment is available for free check-out at the park office. Additionally, there is an accessible fishing pier located in the picnic area along the park's southern shoreline. Due to the rocky nature of the shoreline, Potawatomi Park does not offer a swimming beach. The park's terrain features gently rolling upland areas, encircled by steep slopes and rugged limestone cliffs. In accordance with Wisconsin State Parks hunting and trapping regulations, hunting and trapping are permitted in the park's open areas.

DATE(S) VISITED .... ☐ SPRING ☐ SUMMER ☐ FALL ☐ WINTER

LODGING .... ☐ ☀ ☐ ☁ ☐ 🌧 ☐ ⛅ ☐ ❄

WHO I WENT WITH .... FEE(S) .... PARK HOURS .... TEMP:.........

WILL I RETURN? YES / NO .... RATING ☆ ☆ ☆ ☆ ☆

NOTES

PASSPORT STAMPS

RIB MOUNTAIN STATE PARK

COUNTY	ESTABLISHED	AREA (AC/HA)
MARATHON	1927	1,528 / 618

Rib Mountain, a billion-year-old geological formation, stands as one of Earth's oldest geological features. The park is a superb location for day use, featuring amenities like picnic areas, hiking trails, a picturesque amphitheater, an indoor gathering space, and picnic shelters. From the park's summit, visitors are treated to breathtaking panoramic views of the Wausau region and the Wisconsin River. On the north face of the mountain, you'll find the Granite Peak Ski Resort, which offers downhill skiing and snowboarding. Rib Mountain boasts over 13 miles of hiking trails, with more than eight miles being accessible to individuals with disabilities. The park allows pets on its trails as long as they are leashed with an 8-foot lead. There are no groomed cross-country ski trails within the park, but winter hiking and snowshoeing are permitted in most park areas. One popular option is the 2-mile groomed snowshoe trail, part of the Middle Yellow Trail loop, which can be accessed from the parking lot south of the entrance station. Picnicking is a beloved activity at Rib Mountain. The park provides several picnic areas equipped with tables, two playgrounds, shelters available for reservation, and an amphitheater also available for reservation at the park's summit. It's important to note that pets are not allowed in the picnic areas. Hunting and trapping are permitted in the park's open areas following the hunting and trapping regulations outlined by Wisconsin State Parks.

DATE(S) VISITED .... ☐ SPRING ☐ SUMMER ☐ FALL ☐ WINTER

LODGING .... ☐☼ ☐☁ ☐🌧 ☐🌫 ☐❄

WHO I WENT WITH .... FEE(S) .... PARK HOURS .... TEMP:.........

WILL I RETURN? YES / NO   RATING ☆ ☆ ☆ ☆ ☆

NOTES

PASSPORT STAMPS

RICHARD BONG STATE RECREATION AREA

COUNTY	ESTABLISHED	AREA (AC/HA)
KENOSHA	1963	4,515 / 1,827

Originally intended to be a jet fighter base, Richard Bong State Recreation Area takes its name from Major Richard I. Bong, a native of Poplar, Wisconsin, who held the distinction of being America's top air ace during World War II. This recreation area features an extensive network of 16 miles of hiking trails, allowing visitors to immerse themselves in the local wildlife. Activities like swimming, boating, kayaking, and fishing are available, and there's a spacious 200-foot beach. Additionally, the recreation area provides a boat launch, but it's designated for electric motors only. You can also enjoy shore fishing at Wolf Lake and the city fish pond, but be sure to have a valid Wisconsin fishing license. Richard Bong State Recreation Area offers two family campgrounds, with a total of 217 campsites, including 54 with electric hookups. For group camping, six campsites are available, accommodating up to 225 campers. There's even a cabin designed with specific features to cater to the needs of people with disabilities. Moreover, the park is a fantastic choice for winter camping, with its trail network transforming into scenic cross-country ski trails. Kids can also have a blast sledding. If you're a mountain biking enthusiast, you'll find 8.3 miles of mountain bike trails in the prairie area. For off-road biking, there are trails situated north of Highway 142. Richard Bong State Recreation Area offers a wide range of recreational activities, including high-power rocketry, dogsledding, falconry, ATV sports, land sailing, horseback riding, hunting, and ultralight aviation. The property boasts nearly 6.5 miles of ATV trails and almost 8 miles of off-highway motorcycle trails. There are four different picnic sites on the property, each equipped with picnic tables. The area also features a playground and volleyball nets near the swimming beach, as well as six shelters and an amphitheater available for reservation between May and October. During the winter, cross-country skiing, sledding, and ice fishing are popular sports. However, it's important to note that the trails are not groomed for cross-country skiing. Richard Bong State Recreation Area is designated as a Managed Hunt property.

DATE(S) VISITED .... ☐ SPRING ☐ SUMMER ☐ FALL ☐ WINTER

LODGING .... ☐ ☀ ☐ ☁ ☐ 🌧 ☐ ⛆ ☐ ❄

WHO I WENT WITH .... FEE(S) .... PARK HOURS .... TEMP:.........

WILL I RETURN? YES / NO   RATING ☆ ☆ ☆ ☆ ☆

NOTES

PASSPORT STAMPS

ROCHE-A-CRI STATE PARK

COUNTY	ESTABLISHED	AREA (AC/HA)
ADAMS	1948	604 / 244

The name "Roche-A-Cri" originates from French words meaning "screaming rock." This park is centered around a 300-foot rock outcrop that contains Native American petroglyphs and pictographs. It's the only Native American rock art site in the state. An access ramp leads to an interpretive exhibit showcasing ancient bird symbols and a painting featuring a man and a thunderbird, one of the local deities. Roche-A-Cri State Park boasts over 6 miles of hiking trails, with the highlight being the stairway to the top of the 300-foot Roche-A-Cri mound, offering breathtaking views. The park also features a rustic family campground open from late spring to early fall. There are three picnic areas within the park: one near the park office, another at the steps leading to the mound, and a third at the path to Chickadee Rock. Additionally, there's a picnic shelter available for reservations located near the steps leading to the mound. The primary picnic shelter is situated in a paved picnic area near the office parking lot and is handicap accessible. Playground equipment can be found near the picnic area at the park office, campground, and kiosk, while there are also volleyball and horseshoe pitches nearby. Anglers can try their luck at Carter Creek, where they might find brook trout. During the winter, visitors can enjoy snowshoeing and cross-country skiing on the park's trails. Note that the main entrance is closed in the winter, so visitors should park in the parking lot located on the north side of Czech Avenue, west of State Highway 13. Hunting and trapping are allowed in open areas of the park, following Wisconsin State Parks hunting and trapping regulations.

DATE(S) VISITED .... ☐ SPRING ☐ SUMMER ☐ FALL ☐ WINTER

LODGING .... ☐ ☼ ☐ ☁ ☐ 🌧 ☐ ⛅ ☐ ❄

WHO I WENT WITH .... FEE(S) .... PARK HOURS .... TEMP:.........

WILL I RETURN? YES / NO   RATING ☆ ☆ ☆ ☆ ☆

NOTES

PASSPORT STAMPS

ROCK ISLAND STATE PARK

COUNTY	ESTABLISHED	AREA (AC/HA)
DOOR	1965	912 / 369

This park is situated on Rock Island in Lake Michigan, located at the tip of the Door Peninsula. The primary mode of public transportation to the island is the Karfi passenger ferry departing from Washington Island. However, for those with their own boats, mooring and docking facilities are available, and the island is also accessible by snowmobile and on foot during the winter. It's important to exercise caution as Lake Michigan can be treacherous due to reefs and storms, and dock space is limited and cannot be reserved. Kayaking and canoeing are popular activities around the island, but it's crucial to be aware that lake conditions can change rapidly, leading to dangerous wind and waves. During the early part of the season, particularly in May and June, the cold water poses a specific risk of hypothermia. Visitors are allowed to pull their canoes and kayaks ashore near the campgrounds. Registration at the visitor point of contact is necessary for campers to access the campgrounds. Rock Island State Park offers primitive walk-in campsites, where all supplies must be carried in and out by campers. No vehicles are permitted on Rock Island. Fishing at Rock Island State Park requires a fishing license, with smallmouth bass and gobies being the most frequently caught fish. Bass season in the waters surrounding the islands opens on July 1. There are approximately 10 miles of trails and 6 miles of shoreline available for hiking on the island, and all trails are open to hikers. Several shorter trails connect the campgrounds to the recreation area near the ferry landing and boathouse. Near the boathouse, you'll find a spacious playfield and picnic area with tables and grills. Rock Island boasts one of the most picturesque sand beaches in Door County, with the water being regularly tested for safety. Swimming is permitted along the entire coast, except for the area near the boat dock. Many campers enjoy swimming from the cobble shores close to their campsites.

Notable attractions on the island include the stone Viking boathouse and various structures, including a historic water tower constructed by inventor Chester H. Thordarson, situated within what is now recognized as the Thordarson Estate Historic District. Additionally, visitors can explore Native American artifacts and visit Pottawatomie Light, which holds the distinction of being Wisconsin's oldest lighthouse. Hunting and trapping are allowed in open areas of the park, following the regulations set forth in Wisconsin State Parks for hunting and trapping.

DATE(S) VISITED .... ☐ SPRING ☐ SUMMER ☐ FALL ☐ WINTER

LODGING .... ☐ ☼ ☐ ☁ ☐ 🌧 ☐ 🌫 ☐ ❄

WHO I WENT WITH .... FEE(S) .... PARK HOURS .... TEMP:.........

WILL I RETURN? YES / NO   RATING ☆ ☆ ☆ ☆ ☆

PASSPORT STAMPS

ROCKY ARBOR STATE PARK

COUNTY	ESTABLISHED	AREA (AC/HA)
JUNEAU	1932	244 / 91

Established with the primary purpose of preserving the 500-million-year-old sandstone formations that shape a nearby gorge, this state park is enveloped by ancient rock structures, lush woodlands, and a gently flowing stream. It's an ideal destination for nature enthusiasts, offering a 1-mile nature trail that winds through the park. While exploring this trail, you may have the chance to spot a variety of wildlife, including deer, raccoons, squirrels, bats, and chipmunks. Rocky Arbor State Park provides wooded campsites, with a family campground operational from Memorial Day Weekend to Labor Day Weekend. This campground encompasses 89 campsites nestled within the woods and is equipped with facilities such as showers and flush toilets. Moreover, a number of campsites offer electrical hookups for added convenience. For those looking to enjoy a picnic, there's a designated picnic area and a playground located near the park's entrance, positioned downhill from the campground. The park welcomes visitors year-round, making it suitable for winter activities like hiking and snowshoeing. In addition, the park allows hunting and trapping in its open areas, provided visitors adhere to the hunting and trapping regulations specified by Wisconsin State Parks.

DATE(S) VISITED .... ☐ SPRING ☐ SUMMER ☐ FALL ☐ WINTER

LODGING .... ☐☀ ☐☁ ☐🌧 ☐🌫 ☐❄

WHO I WENT WITH .... FEE(S) .... PARK HOURS .... TEMP:.........

WILL I RETURN? YES / NO   RATING ☆ ☆ ☆ ☆ ☆

NOTES

PASSPORT STAMPS

SAUK PRAIRIE STATE RECREATION AREA

COUNTY	ESTABLISHED	AREA (AC/HA)
SAUK	2004	3,391 / 1,372

The Sauk Prairie State Recreation Area has a unique historical background, as it was formerly a military munitions factory that played a significant role during World War II, the Korean War, and the Vietnam War. At its peak, it held the distinction of being the largest munitions factory in the world during World War II. However, as the military's requirements changed over time, the facility became surplus to their needs. Subsequently, the property was transferred to the state and other proprietors, with the primary focus shifting towards recreational, conservation, and research purposes. Visitors to the area can partake in a diverse range of activities, including biking on the trails, off-road hiking, bird watching, and cross-country skiing. The recreational opportunities extend to hunting, trapping, hiking, mushroom and berry picking, nature observation, photography, and various other conventional outdoor pursuits. Horseback riding is also permitted on the open roads within the complex, provided visitors adhere to posted regulations and exercise caution regarding closed-off areas and potential hazards due to construction debris and dismantled structures. The Sauk Prairie State Recreation Area welcomes visitors year-round, operating from one hour before sunrise to one hour after sunset. During the winter season, it's important to note that the roads are not plowed or maintained for snow and ice, so individuals planning to visit during this period should be prepared accordingly.

DATE(S) VISITED .... ☐ SPRING ☐ SUMMER ☐ FALL ☐ WINTER

LODGING .... ☐ ☼ ☐ ☁ ☐ 🌧 ☐ ⛈ ☐ ❄

WHO I WENT WITH .... FEE(S) .... PARK HOURS .... TEMP:........

WILL I RETURN? YES / NO   RATING ☆ ☆ ☆ ☆ ☆

NOTES

PASSPORT STAMPS

STRAIGHT LAKE STATE PARK

COUNTY	ESTABLISHED	AREA (AC/HA)
POLK	2002	2,000 / 809

The park features a network of trails that provide breathtaking vistas of the lakes and glaciers within the area. On the southern side of the park, there are ten campgrounds, boat launch sites, and a picnic area, which can be reserved in advance. Visitors should keep in mind the park's policy of "carry-in/carry-out," meaning that they are responsible for removing any waste they generate, and should bring their own water supply. The park is designated for pedestrian use only, with no allowance for motorized vehicles, bicycles, or horses. Notably, the Ice Age National Scenic Trail runs through the central part of the park, closely following the course of the Straight River and Straight Lake. The park boasts approximately 8.5 miles of trails, including the Clam Falls Trail, an abandoned road that played a pivotal role during the logging era and runs parallel to the Ice Age Trail. Bird enthusiasts will find the park an excellent spot for bird watching. Straight Lake State Park offers an array of recreational opportunities. Furthermore, the park shares a border with a state wilderness area, resulting in a contiguous expanse of almost 3,500 acres. Straight Lake is both fed and drained by the Straight River and is renowned for being one of the premier northern wild lakes, providing exceptional fishing for perch, northern pike, and various panfish. Anglers can access the lake by boat, and Rainbow Lake, which is stocked with rainbow trout annually, offers trout fishing from the first Saturday in May to the first Sunday in March. A fishing dock can be found at Rainbow Lake near the boat landing. Note that individuals aged 16 or older are required to have a valid fishing license. During the winter season, the trails are not groomed or paved, but visitors are permitted to partake in winter hiking, snowshoeing, and cross-country skiing throughout the park. Furthermore, hunting and trapping are allowed in designated open areas of the park in accordance with Wisconsin State Parks' hunting and trapping regulations.

DATE(S) VISITED ....

☐ SPRING   ☐ SUMMER   ☐ FALL   ☐ WINTER

LODGING ....

☐ ☀   ☐ ☁   ☐ 🌧   ☐ 🌫   ☐ ❄

WHO I WENT WITH ....

FEE(S) .... PARK HOURS .... TEMP:........

WILL I RETURN? YES / NO

RATING ☆ ☆ ☆ ☆ ☆

NOTES

PASSPORT STAMPS

TOWER HILL STATE PARK

COUNTY	ESTABLISHED	AREA (AC/HA)
IOWA	1922	77 / 31

The park is home to the meticulously reconstructed Helena Shot Tower, a historic structure with a rich past. The original shot tower, which was completed in 1832, played a crucial role in manufacturing lead shot until the year 1860. Visitors to the park can witness the fascinating process of how lead shot was produced in the mid-1800s. In addition to the historical site, there are bluff trails that offer excellent hiking opportunities. Tower Hill State Park provides a range of amenities for visitors to enjoy. These include a picnic area, a spacious playfield, a shelter that can be reserved in advance, a canoe landing on the Wisconsin River, and a campground with ten available campsites. It's important to note that, as of 2019, all campsites within the campground can be reserved. The campground operates during the designated seasonal periods. The park is adjacent to the Wisconsin River, and it shares a border with state-owned land encompassing the Lower Wisconsin State Riverway. While Tower Hill State Park does not have its own boat landing, it is a favored destination for exploration by kayak or canoe. Fishing is another popular activity in the floodplains of the Wisconsin River. For those who enjoy the great outdoors, the park features 2-mile trails that wind through its scenic landscapes. Birdwatching enthusiasts will appreciate the diverse range of habitats found in the park, including riverbanks, dense woods, and open clearings that attract various bird species. In the vicinity of Tower Hill State Park, there are several noteworthy attractions to explore, including Taliesin, the American Players Theatre, the House on the Rock, and Governor Dodge State Park. Lastly, hunting and trapping are permitted in specific open areas of the park, adhering to the hunting and trapping regulations outlined by Wisconsin State Parks.

DATE(S) VISITED ....

LODGING ....

WHO I WENT WITH ....

WILL I RETURN? YES / NO

☐ SPRING ☐ SUMMER ☐ FALL ☐ WINTER

☐ ☀ ☐ ☁ ☐ ☔ ☐ ⛆ ☐ ❄

FEE(S) .... PARK HOURS .... TEMP:.........

RATING ☆ ☆ ☆ ☆ ☆

NOTES

PASSPORT STAMPS

TURTLE-FLAMBEAU SCENIC WATERS AREA

COUNTY	ESTABLISHED	AREA (AC/HA)
IRON	1926	40,000 / 16,187

The Turtle-Flambeau Scenic Waters Area, situated in the wild and rugged northern region of Wisconsin, provides an undisturbed and natural environment characterized by pristine, wooded shorelines and islands. This area offers a wide range of outdoor activities, including boating, camping, fishing, and opportunities to immerse oneself in the great outdoors. Visitors to the Turtle-Flambeau Scenic Waters Area can take advantage of 66 secluded camping sites that are accessible solely by water. Among these sites, the family campsites and two group sites do not require prior registration, fees, or camping permits. Additionally, there are six group sites available for reservation, and these do entail a fee. The sites are available for use year-round and are assigned on a first-come, first-served basis. While camping in the area is free, it is important to adhere to the designated camping sites to protect the natural environment. In the past, this region was home to numerous lakeside resorts. However, today, much of the shoreline remains minimally developed, preserving the area's natural beauty. The Turtle-Flambeau Scenic Waters Area boasts six boat and kayak launch sites situated along the Turtle-Flambeau Flowage River. Additionally, there is a boat launch located in Lake of the Falls County Park at the northern end of the watercourse. The flowage is renowned for its exceptional north woods fishing experiences and supports a diverse range of native warm-water fish species. Anglers can seek walleye, muskellunge, northern pike, smallmouth and largemouth bass, lake sturgeon, and various panfish species. The area features five hiking trails and offers many miles of old logging roads for hiking enthusiasts to explore. The Hidden Rivers Nature Trail, a 2-mile interpretive trail accessible from Fisherman's Landing Road, provides an informative hiking experience. Other trails such as Big Island Trail, Wilson Hills Trail, and Deadhorse Trail are open year-round and suitable for hiking or hunting. The Little Turtle Trail is primarily favored by birdwatchers but is closed to hikers between December 15 and April 15 if the ground is covered with snow, as it is part of the MECCA cross-country trail system. The Turtle-Flambeau Scenic Waters Area's diverse topography, vegetation, and water resources create a prime environment for hunting and trapping. The area is home to a variety of wildlife, including deer, bear, grouse, woodcock, turkey, grey hare, raccoon, coyote, rat, fox, mink, beaver, otter, muskrat, and various waterfowl, providing ample opportunities for outdoor enthusiasts.

NOTES

PASSPORT STAMPS

WHITEFISH DUNES STATE PARK

COUNTY	ESTABLISHED	AREA (AC/HA)
DOOR	1967	867 / 349

Whitefish Dunes State Park serves as a sanctuary for the delicate dune ecosystem in Door County's eastern peninsula. This day-use park offers visitors the opportunity to stroll along the picturesque shores of Lake Michigan or explore the vast dunes and lush forests via a network of trails. The park's nature center hosts year-round programs, educational exhibits, and demonstrations for guests. A variety of recreational activities can be enjoyed at Whitefish Dunes State Park, including hiking, fishing, kayaking, boating, and swimming. During the winter months, the park provides opportunities for skiing and snowshoeing. When snowfall occurs, the red, green, and yellow trails are groomed and suitable for diagonal skiing, while the black trail is designated for snowshoeing. Bicycling is permitted only on specific bike paths, including areas near the park office, the Red Trail leading to S. Cave Point Drive, the Third Beach entrance to Clark Lake Road, and from the office to Schauer Road. It is important to note that biking is not allowed on the beach, dunes, or hiking trails. Whitefish Dunes State Park boasts 14.5 miles of hiking trails, with an emphasis on staying on designated paths and steps to safeguard the rare plant and animal species that inhabit the area. The park also features 1.5 miles of sandy beach, offering a perfect location for leisurely walks, dune viewing, and enjoying the refreshing waters of Lake Michigan. Swimming in Lake Michigan is permitted; however, there are no lifeguards on duty. While there is no boat launch within the park, Clark Lake is available for fishing. The Clark Lake Spur trail provides access to Clark Lake from within the park. A fishing license is required for those looking to fish in this area. Additionally, the park office offers free basic fishing equipment rentals for anglers of all ages. The park's picnic area is equipped with charcoal grills, picnic tables, a reservable shelter building, and a drinking fountain. This picnic spot is conveniently located near the parking lot, offering picturesque views of the Lake Michigan shoreline. Hunting and trapping are allowed in open areas of Whitefish Dunes State Park, provided that visitors adhere to the hunting and trapping regulations set forth by Wisconsin State Parks.

DATE(S) VISITED .... □ SPRING □ SUMMER □ FALL □ WINTER

LODGING .... □ ☼ □ ☁ □ ☔ □ ⛅ □ ❄

WHO I WENT WITH .... FEE(S) .... PARK HOURS .... TEMP:.........

WILL I RETURN? YES / NO RATING ☆ ☆ ☆ ☆ ☆

NOTES

WILDCAT MOUNTAIN STATE PARK

COUNTY	ESTABLISHED	AREA (AC/HA)
VERNON	1948	3,643 / 1,474

Wildcat Mountain State Park is perched on the precipice of a hill, providing a breathtaking vantage point overlooking the grandeur of the Kickapoo River Valley. The Kickapoo River, stretching over 100 miles, stands as the longest tributary of the Wisconsin River. Within the park's confines, visitors will discover a lush forest, the pristine waters of the river, and meandering streams, all set against a stunning backdrop, inviting them to partake in fishing, hiking, and picnicking. The park offers a range of camping options for families, groups, and equestrians. Scenic trails, spanning a total of 21 miles, traverse the park and cater to hikers, nature enthusiasts, and equestrians. Eagle Scouts have contributed two compass orienteering trails, with one covering 1.33 miles and the other 1.05 miles. Compasses can be rented at the park office for those eager to explore these orienteering routes. Wildcat Mountain State Park further features several horse trail loops, totaling 15 miles, and provides 24 horse camping sites, situated northeast of the park office along Taylor Valley Road. It's worth noting that the park does not offer horse rentals for visitors. A lookout point and multiple picnic areas within the park grant visitors panoramic views of the picturesque Kickapoo Valley. The Kickapoo River, renowned for its miles of leisurely flow through unspoiled regions, beckons kayaking enthusiasts, who can rent equipment in the nearby Village of Ontario. Paddlers have the opportunity to observe the rare plant species that flourish along the riverbanks and observe the vibrant wildlife inhabiting the area, including muskrats, banded kingfishers, green herons, and blue herons. The section of the Kickapoo River between Ontario and Gays Mills is home to an impressive 46 fish species, including a bountiful population of brown trout. Visitors of all ages may borrow basic fishing equipment free of charge from the park office. Wildcat Mountain State Park is equipped with an upper picnic area featuring a reservable shelter and a playground. Down by the Kickapoo River, a lower picnic area features an unreservable shelter. Additionally, a picnic area at the Ice Cave trail parking lot offers further opportunities for relaxation. The park is also home to two shelters and an amphitheater, providing space for gatherings and events year-round. In the winter, the park transforms into a snowy wonderland, with seven miles of cross-country ski trails awaiting skiers, who can initiate and conclude their runs at either the park office or maintenance building. The 2.5-mile Old-Settlers hiking trail loop is repurposed into a snowshoe trail during the winter months. Hunting and trapping are permitted in open areas of Wildcat Mountain State Park in accordance with Wisconsin State Parks hunting and trapping regulations.

DATE(S) VISITED .... □ SPRING □ SUMMER □ FALL □ WINTER

LODGING .... □ ☀ □ ☁ □ 🌧 □ ☁ □ ❄

WHO I WENT WITH .... FEE(S) .... PARK HOURS .... TEMP:.........

WILL I RETURN? YES / NO   RATING ☆ ☆ ☆ ☆ ☆

WILLOW RIVER STATE PARK

COUNTY	ESTABLISHED	AREA (AC/HA)
ST. CROIX	1967	2,800 / 1,133

The star attraction of this park is its magnificent waterfall, Willow Falls, which plunges dramatically 200 feet into a deep gorge. Another highly regarded feature is Little Falls Lake, a relatively shallow reservoir located on the Willow River. The gorge's lower layers contain trilobite fossils, suggesting that the rock formation is approximately 600 million years old. Willow River State Park offers a diverse array of recreational activities, including camping, fishing, boating, swimming, rock climbing, biking, and hiking. The park boasts a network of 11 trails, covering a total of more than 13 miles. These trails vary in difficulty to cater to various skill levels. On the north side of the river, the park provides 2 miles of paved trails suitable for pet owners and accommodating activities such as snowshoeing, dog sledding, and hiking. Among the park's hiking trails, Willow Falls is the most sought-after destination, offering mesmerizing views of the river valley. Furthermore, Willow River State Park ensures accessibility with the wheelchair-friendly Hidden Ponds Nature Trail. The park features wheelchair-accessible campsites and a fishing pier. Anglers can expect to find various warm-water species, including panfish, bass, and northern, especially below the dam. Additionally, the Willow River is stocked with trout, with the best trout fishing typically found upstream from the waterfall. Cycling enthusiasts can explore the park via the paved Little Falls Trail, designated single-track mountain bike trails, and the park's roadways. Little Falls Lake boasts a swimming beach for those seeking aquatic relaxation. While the Willow River offers numerous access points, there are no other officially designated swimming areas within the park. Boating, kayaking, and canoeing are popular activities on Little Falls Lake, where a convenient boat landing is situated. Rentals are available during the season. Kayaking on the river is also an option, but kayakers must exercise caution due to fluctuating river conditions and submerged debris. For motorized boating experiences, visitors can explore nearby lakes and the St. Croix River. The park's campground, located on the southern shore of Little Falls Lake, is exceptionally popular and frequently reaches high occupancy rates, making it one of the most sought-after campgrounds within the Wisconsin State Park System. Willow River State Park offers picnic areas replete with tables and grills at various locations throughout the park. The most extensive picnic area is situated at the beach on Little Falls Lake. While pets are not allowed in the beach picnic area, there is a designated pet-friendly area featuring tables and grills at the boat launch. Willow River State Park accommodates families with three separate playgrounds: one at the beach picnic area, another at Campground 100, and the third at Campground 300. The beach picnic area also offers substantial open grassy areas suitable for sports and recreational activities. The park features a shelter near the dam's picnic area, available for reservations, and another shelter at the beach area, which operates on a first-come, first-served basis. Hunting and trapping are permitted in the park's open areas in accordance with the regulations governing hunting and trapping in Wisconsin State Parks.

DATE(S) VISITED .... ☐ SPRING ☐ SUMMER ☐ FALL ☐ WINTER

LODGING .... ☐ ☀ ☐ ☁ ☐ 🌧 ☐ 🌫 ☐ ❄

WHO I WENT WITH .... FEE(S) .... PARK HOURS .... TEMP:.........

WILL I RETURN? YES / NO   RATING ☆ ☆ ☆ ☆ ☆

NOTES

PASSPORT STAMPS

WYALUSING STATE PARK

COUNTY	ESTABLISHED	AREA (AC/HA)
GRANT	1917	2,628 / 1,064

The name "Wyalusing" derives from the Lenape language, spoken by the Munsee-Delaware tribes who settled in the area during the 19th century after being displaced from farther east. Wyalusing State Park, famous for its dramatic, steep bluffs that offer panoramic views, is situated at the confluence of the Mississippi and Wisconsin Rivers. These bluffs rise over 500 feet above the river valley and are a haven for birdwatchers, boasting a diverse population of more than 90 bird species. The park features two mountain bike trails, Whitetail Meadows and Mississippi Ridge, which are not intended for high-speed riding. These trails can become soft and slippery when wet and may erode quickly during heavy rains. There is a boat landing within the park that provides access for launching boats, including motorized ones. Additionally, nearby companies in Bagley and the Prairie du Chien area offer boat rentals. While the park itself lacks a beach, you can find a beach, boat landing, and picnic area at Wyalusing Recreation Area, located 2 miles to the south of the park entrance. Another option is the municipal swimming area in Prairie du Chien. A unique way to explore the river floodplains is by canoe, which allows you to observe waterfowl, aquatic plants, and a variety of bottom-dwelling animals. The canoe trail begins and ends at the park's boat landing. The backwaters of the Mississippi and Wisconsin rivers provide excellent fishing opportunities for a variety of species, including panfish, bass, northern pike, and walleye. An accessible fishing pier is available at the boat landing. Wyalusing State Park offers several camping choices, such as two family campsites, an outdoor group camp, and the Hugh Harper indoor group camp. The park boasts over 14 miles of hiking trails, which vary in difficulty. There are several picnic areas and shelters within the park, with the central picnic area located near the entrance to the Wisconsin Ridge campground. Picnic spots include the Peterson shelter, as well as the playground across from it, the Homestead picnic area, the Henneger Point picnic area, and the Green Cloud picnic area. At the entrance to the Wisconsin Ridge campground, you'll find a playground for children. For group activities, the park provides five open shelters that can be reserved. In the winter, Wyalusing State Park offers a range of cross-country ski trails suitable for all skill levels, all accessible from the Astronomy Center parking lot. These trails include Turkey Hollow, Whitetail Meadows, and Prairie. Cross-country skiers can enjoy picturesque vistas of the mighty Mississippi River from Cathedral Tree Drive. Hunting and trapping are allowed in the open areas of the park, following the regulations stipulated by the Wisconsin State Parks for hunting and trapping.

NOTES

_____
_____
_____
_____
_____
_____
_____
_____
_____
_____
_____
_____
_____
_____
_____
_____
_____
_____
_____
_____
_____
_____
_____
_____

PASSPORT STAMPS

YELLOWSTONE LAKE STATE PARK

COUNTY	ESTABLISHED	AREA (AC/HA)
LAFAYETTE	1970	968 / 392

Yellowstone Lake State Park is a popular year-round recreational destination, offering a wide range of activities for visitors, including camping, swimming, fishing, boating, hiking, biking, and picnicking. During the winter months, the park remains open for ice fishing, snowmobiling, and cross-country skiing. The neighboring Yellowstone Wildlife Area also provides additional recreational opportunities, such as horseback riding trails and a shooting range. The park features 4 miles of off-road bicycle trails, but it's important to note that the park's roads and trails are frequently used by various visitors, so bicyclists should exercise caution, be aware of other park users, and watch for both traffic and pedestrians. Yellowstone Lake, covering 455 acres, is accessible for various watercraft, including boats, canoes, kayaks, sailboats, and more. There are two boat launch ramps and a dedicated kayak launch area. At the eastern end of the lake, you'll find a food court and a boat rental facility, available during the summer season. The lake also features a designated swimming beach, and a bathhouse is located nearby; however, it's important to note that there are no lifeguards on duty. Yellowstone Lake State Park provides both family and group campsites, accommodating various types of camping experiences. The lake is renowned for its thriving populations of crappies, walleye, and other gamefish. Anglers can also find opportunities to catch bass, bluegill, channel catfish, muskies, and northern pike in the lake. With over 13 miles of hiking trails, the park offers numerous options for hikers, though the trails can vary in difficulty and may include steep climbs, descents, and stairways. The primary trailhead is situated at the base of Campground Hill Road. Visitors can enjoy picnicking at nine designated areas within the park, including a picnic shelter at the west end of the lake that can be reserved for special events. It's important to follow the "carry in, carry out" rule since there are no trash or recycling bins in the day use or picnic areas. Pets are not allowed in the picnic areas, beach zones, or playgrounds, but there are designated pet areas located to the west of the beach. Cross-country skiing enthusiasts can take advantage of 5 miles of groomed and maintained trails within the park, though their availability depends on weather conditions and available personnel. While a Wisconsin State Park trail pass is not required at Yellowstone Lake, a vehicle sticker is necessary for entry to the park. Hunting and trapping are permitted in open areas of the park, adhering to the regulations set forth by Wisconsin State Parks governing hunting and trapping activities.

DATE(S) VISITED .... ☐ SPRING ☐ SUMMER ☐ FALL ☐ WINTER

LODGING .... ☐ ☀ ☐ ☁ ☐ 🌧 ☐ 🌨 ☐ ❄

WHO I WENT WITH .... FEE(S) .... PARK HOURS .... TEMP:.........

WILL I RETURN? YES / NO   RATING ☆ ☆ ☆ ☆ ☆

PASSPORT STAMPS

PHOTOS   PARK NAME..

PHOTOS   PARK NAME...

PHOTOS   PARK NAME...

PHOTOS   PARK NAME...

PHOTOS　　　　PARK NAME..

PHOTOS   PARK NAME...

PHOTOS

PARK NAME..

PHOTOS   PARK NAME...

PHOTOS   PARK NAME...

PHOTOS   PARK NAME..

Thank you for taking the time to read our book. We hope you found it enjoyable.

Your feedback is important to us, and we would greatly appreciate it if you could take a moment to share your thoughts by leaving an online review.

Your review will not only help us improve as an author but also assist other potential readers in making informed decisions.

Once again, thank you for your support and for considering leaving a review.

Write to us if you think we should improve anything in our book:

y4.publishing@gmail.com

SEE OTHER BOOKS

MISSOURI
STATE PARKS
BUCKET LIST

NEW YORK
STATE PARKS
BUCKET LIST

OHIO
STATE PARKS
BUCKET LIST

PENNSYLVANIA
STATE PARKS
BUCKET LIST

TENNESSEE
STATE PARKS
BUCKET LIST

TEXAS
STATE PARKS
BUCKET LIST

UTAH
STATE PARKS
BUCKET LIST

VIRGINIA
STATE PARKS
BUCKET LIST

WASHINGTON
STATE PARKS
BUCKET LIST

Made in the USA
Monee, IL
20 October 2024

68357742R00085